Those Valiant Texans -
Texans -
A Breed Apart

Those Valiant Texans - A Breed Apart

by Robert M. Bartlett

Peter E. Randall
PUBLISHER

Cover and title page sketches by Jan Norton.

Peter E. Randall Publisher
Box 4726, Portsmouth, NH 03801

Library of Congress Cataloging-in-Publication Data

Bartlett, Robert Merrill
　　Those Valiant Texans : a breed apart / by Robert M. Bartlett.
　　　　p.　　cm. ·
　　Bibliography: p.
　　ISBN 0-914339-26-5
　　1. Hill, John Christopher Columbus. 1828–1904. 2. Santa Anna,
Antonio López de, 1794?–1876. 3. Texas--History--Revolution,
1835–1836--Campaigns. 4. Pioneers--Texas--Biography. 5. Americans--
Mexico--Biography. 6. Hill family. I. Title.
F390.H58B37　1989
976.4'03'0922--dc19　　　　　　　　　　　　　　　　　　　89-30602
　　　　　　　　　　　　　　　　　　　　　　　　　　　　　　CIP

To
Eugenia Theresa Hill,
great-granddaughter of Asa and Elizabeth Hill,
born and raised in La Grange, Texas.

Mother of Sue Nuckols Bartlett.

Other books by Robert M. Bartlett

The Call of the Phoenix: Vignettes of Old and New China
My Corner of New England
Pilgrim House by the Sea
The Pilgrim Way
The Faith of the Pilgrims
Thanksgiving Day
They Stand Invincible: Men Who are Reshaping Our World
Sky Pioneer: The Story of Igor I. Sikorsky
They Dared to Live
They Dared to Believe
The Great Empire of Silence
Builders of a New World

Illustrations

Eugenia Theresa Hill Nuckols, great granddaughter of Asa. (Hill family records.)   v

Sam Houston. (Courtesy Texas State Library.)   8

The Hill School House as it looked in 1907. Building date unknown. (Courtesy *Fayette County Record*.)   16

Elizabeth Barksdale Hill, mother of John Christopher Columbus Hill. (Hill family records.)   19

General Thomas Jefferson Green. (Courtesy Texas State Library.)   35

John Christopher Columbus Hill breaking his rifle. (courtesy Texas State Library.)   62

General Pedro De Ampudia. (Courtesy University of Texas at Austin.)   68

Archbishop Manuel Posada. (Courtesy University of Texas at Austin.)   90

General Antonio Lopez de Santa Anna. (Courtesy Texas State Library.)   98

Big Foot Wallace. (Courtesy Texas State Library.)   108

Drawing of the Black Beans. (Courtesy Museum of Fine Arts, Houston, painting by Frederick Remington.)   111

The National Palace of Mexico. (Courtesy University of Texas at Austin.)   123

Texan prisoners repairing roadway at the palace of Archbishop Manuel Posada. (Courtesy Texas State Library.)   131

General Jose Marie Tormel. (Courtesy University
of Texas at Austin.)   156

John Christopher Columbus Hill as a young man in
Mexico City. (Courtesy Library of Texas.)   159

John Christopher Columbus Hill with his daughter
Maclovia and her two daughters. (Hill family
records.)   176

Green Washington Hill, age 21, son of Dr. Green
Washington Hill, grandson of Asa Hill, grandfather
of Sue Nuckols Bartlett. (Hill family records.)   189

Virginia Nuckols Cason, age 18, great-great-
granddaughter of Asa Hill, sister of Sue Nuckols
Bartlett, pioneer educator. (Hill family records.)   198

Memorial to the Texas Veterans at the Monument
Hill Park, La Grange, Texas. (Photograph by Mary
Bartlett Reynolds.)   207

Contents

Acknowledgments   xi
Introduction   xiii

1   Arrival of the Hills   1
2   War Clouds   5
3   Another Summons   13
4   Impatient Volunteers   26
5   Impending Encounter   37
6   A Daring Venture   47
7   The Young Hero Confronts
      General Ampudia   64
8   Deceit and Humiliation   73
9   John's Survival in Mexico City   89
10   Drawing of the Black Beans   103
11   Grim Perote Prison   118
12   The Incorrigible Texans   136
13   The Fall of Santa Anna   151
14   Engineer, Entrepreneur, Physician   160
15   The Hill Family Saga   177
16   Light Along the Path   190
17   Remembering the Patriots   199

Letter   208
Notes   212

Acknowledgments

Gratitude is expressed to the Archives of the Texas State Library, the Eugene E. Baker History Center and the Institute of Texan Culture at San Antonio for their help in obtaining photographs.

Appreciation is extended to my wife, Sue, and other members of the Hill family.

I wish to thank numerous others who have helped: the Texas University Library, the Texas State Library, the Institute of Texan Culture at San Antonio, the Eugene C. Baker History Center, Houston Public Library, the *Fayette County Record*, La Grange, the San Jacinto Museum Association, the University of Georgia Library, Harvard University Library, Yale University Library, Plymouth Public Library, Plymouth, Massachusetts, Collier County Public Library, Naples, Florida, Southern Methodist University Library and San Antonio Public Library, and the Museum of Fine Arts, Houston.

Sue and I give special thanks to her cousin, Joseph E. Blanton, distinguished scholar and rancher of Albany, Texas, great-great-grandson of Asa and Elizabeth Barksdale Hill, formally on the faculty of the University of Texas. He has delved deeply into the annals of the Hill–Kerr–Webb and Blanton families.

Thanks are extended to him for permission to use material from his collection of letters from John C. C. Hill and Lucy Hill Jones and *The Romance of John C. C. Hill and Mary Muray* by Lucy Hill Jones.

We also thank the Texas State Library and the Texas State Archives for permission to use the letters

xi

of John C. C. Hill and William G. Webb collection. The Spanish letters were translated by Alinda De Franco Cato.

Page footnotes indicate the reference sources and book references. They are listed at the back of the book.

Introduction

My wife, Sue, is a Texan, born and bred, a great-great-grandaughter of Asa Hill and a grandniece of John Christopher Columbus Hill, the meteoric luminary of the Hill family.

For years I have listened to the exploits of this achiever, hoping one day to publish his story. I am not writing an academic book but rather the account of a typical Texas pioneer family—Asa and Elizabeth Barksdale Hill and their twelve children. I try to recount the character and spirit of the Hills, their cousins, neighbors and friends—like the Kerrs, Webbs and Blantons.

The family is unique not only for its size but for its Methodist faith and dedication to the ideals of the American Constitution. Hardy and venturesome, they established foundation values in the new world of the Southwest.

I have studied the primary sources preserved by Hill scholars such as George A. Hill, Jr., Luther Henry Hill, Joseph E. Blanton, Lucy Hill Jones, William G. Webb and Sue's mother, Eugenia Theresa Hill Nuckols.

There were also gifted writers who kept journals of this period of conflict between Texas and Mexico. They include Thomas Jefferson Green, William P. Stapp, Hugh Kerr, Israel Canfield, James A. Glascock, Thomas W. Bell, Waddy Thompson and others to whom we are deeply indebted.

One biography of John Christopher Columbus Hill was published in 1909, *The Boy Captive of the*

Mier Expedition, by Fanny Chambers Gooch Iglehart by the Passing Show Publishing Company, San Antonio, Texas. Impressed by her writing on Mexico, John C. C. Hill visited her in her home in Austin and recounted to her the story of his adventuresome life.

He said, "I have had a very remarkable and romantic career and have often been solicited by writers to give them the story of my life, but I never consented because they were seeking only to make money. But you have demonstrated beyond all doubt your noble friendship for the Mexican people and I am glad to tell you all about it, for sometime you may want to make it into a book for the benefit and pleasure of the children of Texas. If you will get a pencil and tablet I will talk while you write."[1]

The dialogue she recorded was not fictionized but authentic conversations between him and General Ampudia, Archbishop Posada, President Santa Anna, General Tornel and others.

John, youngest of the Hill children, took the stage at the age of thirteen and played a commanding role in the tumultuous events of Mexico and Texas for over fifty years!

Many hitherto unpublished family letters, biographical and historical materials, are included in this book.

Robert M. Bartlett
34 Brook Road, RFD 1
Plymouth, Massachusetts 02360

1

Arrival of the Hills

*A*SA HILL AND HIS WIFE, Elizabeth Barksdale, were illustrious figures in early Texas history. Asa was born in Martin County, North Carolina, circa 1788, the son of Isaac Hill and Lucy Wallace Hill and was one of ten children. They lived not far from Fayetteville and La Grange, Georgia.

The family of Isaac Hill moved to Georgia and established the town of Hillsborough near another La Grange and Fayetteville. The Hills were a part of that generation who admired the Marquis de La Fayette and named settlements in his honor.

In Georgia Asa Hill married Elizabeth Barksdale October 6, 1808. They had twelve children who lived to maturity. One child died in infancy.

The six Hill sons were:

Green Washington
William Carol Andrew Jackson
Jeffrey Barksdale
James Monroe
Asa Collingsworth
John Christopher Columbus

The six daughters were:

Serena Pinkney (married George A. Kerr)
Susanna Amanda (married Rev. C. W. Thomas)
Louisiana Elizabeth (married William Penn Kerr)
Mary Anne Rebecca (married Peter B. Shaw)
Sarah Anne Amelia (married General
William G. Webb)
Martha Anne Eliza[1]

It is evident that Asa and Elizabeth did not intend their children to grow up as any Tom, Dick or Jane. They were to be achievers.

The parents of these two remarkable people were of hardy English and Scottish stock who had large and rugged families.

My wife, Sue, a descendant of Asa and Elizabeth Hill, and now 89 years of age, remembers great aunts and uncles in their nineties, still hale and hearty, enjoying family gatherings, eating fried chicken, sweet corn and watermelon like the rest.

Sue says she cut her teeth on stories of the Hill family, especially John Christopher Columbus, the Boy Captive. Her mother, Eugenia Theresa Hill Nuckols, was a natural historian and passed on to her daughter all her photographs and mementoes of the family. Sue zealously guarded these treasures and kept them tied up in small beribboned packages in her little tin trunk bound by wooden slats. Inside is a tray with two compartments, the smaller one having a lid, and there she kept the priceless photographs of Elizabeth Barksdale Hill, John Christopher Columbus, his daughter and grandchildren, great aunts and uncles and cousins.[2]

In 1824 Mexico initiated a colonization plan, inviting foreigners to settle in that vast, empty area where they were to be free from taxes for ten years. Each family was granted 4,428 acres of land for a thirty-dollar fee. Impresarios were appointed to handle the new colonies. Stephen Austin, who had been given a grant, issued notices in the newspapers in the States and "Texas fever" began.

In 1834 Asa Hill, accompanied by his son, William Carol Andrew Jackson and his nephew, Isaac La Fayette, journeyed to Austin to select a place for a permanent settlement in Austin's colony near Gay Head. They then returned to Georgia to arrange for the removal of the family to Texas.[3]

John Christopher Columbus was seven years old when the Hills started on a steamboat journey down the Chattahoochee River to the port of Apalachicola where they took a schooner for New Orleans. Transferring to a sailing vessel, they endured a stormy voyage of eighteen days to Matagorda on Matagorda Bay. There they secured ox wagons and traveled on to San Felipe, which was at that time the seat of the provincial government.

They camped at night with other travelers. The men shot deer and antelope. After a journey of seven days they reached Gay Head, their final destination.[4]

Immediately all set to work to cut down trees, build a house and barn, split rails and set up fences, break the land and sow their crops.

The newcomers did not realize all the serious problems that had evolved between the settlers and Mexico. President Santa Anna had altered the original agreements and imposed many restrictions. This angered the settlers, who resisted the orders and defended their rights. The Texans had no organized army to face the powerful Mexican forces.

2

War Clouds

*S*HORTLY AFTER THE ARRIVAL of the Hills in Gay
Head, news spread of the siege of the Alamo,
once an old Spanish mission, now used by the Texans
as a garrison. Asa and William Carol Andrew Jackson
set out with their rifles to aid the defenders, but
arrived too late.

Travis, Bowie, Crockett and their company of
187 men from many states of the Union took their
stand against 1,800 of Santa Anna's troops. The Texans were massacred March 6, 1836 and their bodies
burned. Great wooden pyres were built and grease
applied. It took two days to consume the corpses.

The reports of Santa Anna's brutalities spread
through Texas and the United States, arousing the people to condemn him as a "butcher" and "bloody tiger."

On March 1, 1836, just five days before the fall
of the Alamo, Texan delegates had assembled in the
frontier village of Washington—on the Brazos—and
on the second day signed their declaration of independence, using an eagle feather to affix their signa-
tures. David Burnet was elected president; Lorenzo
de Zavala, one of the most cultivated men in the terri-

tory, was elected vice president and Sam Houston was made head of the army.[1]

When Houston reached Gonzalas he decided not to move on to San Antonio, but to fall back. He ordered Fannin to move his troops from Goliad to the east and lure the enemy deeper into Texas, further from their supplies.

Fannin delayed in following Houston's orders. Consequently he was surprised some ten miles east of Goliad by Santa Anna's General Josè Urrea. Fannin's 400 men fought bravely but were overwhelmed by the Mexicans' larger and better equipped forces.

The Texans raised the white flag and, after a parley, were told that if they surrendered they would be treated as prisoners of war and sent to New Orleans by ship. Following this agreement, the Texans laid down their muskets and were led back to Goliad and locked up in a church for a week.

On Palm Sunday, March 27, they were ordered out of their confinement, believing that they were going home but instead were shot, bayonetted, piled together, covered with brush and oil and burned.

To pursue the troops of Houston, Santa Anna divided his forces, assuming the lead himself. He crossed the Colorado and took San Felipe to discover that Houston was close at hand.

When Santa Anna learned that President Burnet and his government were near, he swooped in at night only to discover that the officials had fled. He burned the place and pushed on until he found himself in a triangular area formed by the San Jacinto River, the Buffalo Bayou and Vince's Bayou.

Sam Houston requested his old friend, Asa

Hill, to serve as a special messenger, speeding on horseback to the east, warning the people to keep out of the path of the Mexican army. Thus he escaped the battle of San Jacinto. However, his son, James Monroe, one of the youthful volunteers, fought in this battle that changed history.

General Houston told his men that their arch foe was at hand: "Victory is certain. Trust in God and fear not. And remember the Alamo. Remember Goliad."

The Mexican leader, General Cos, suggested that his weary men be permitted a siesta. He retired to his marquee while the commander dozed under a great oak. Houston drew up his 783 men. At four o'clock on April 21, 1836, he lifted his sword, mounted his horse and led the attack. The Texans ran forward under the live oaks, trailing with moss, and through the high prairie grass. The Mexicans were confident that there would be no fight that day. Their horses were not saddled; their twelve-pound gun was unloaded. Washing hung by tents and trees, while the camp dozed blissfully.[2]

The two new six-pounders that had just arrived as a gift to the Lone Star Republic from Cincinnati, Ohio, boomed. The Texans knelt and fired their muskets. Then shouting "Remember the Alamo!," they rushed ahead, clubbing their guns and grasping their bowie knives. In eighteen brief minutes the Battle of San Jacinto was over. During the riot that followed many of the Mexicans fell on their knees, crying, "Me no Alamo. Me no Alamo!"

Santa Anna fled toward Vince's Bayou where the foresighted Houston had destroyed the bridge.

Sam Houston.
(Courtesy San Jacinto Museum of History Association.)

The bayou was full of wounded and drowned men. Seizing the Mexican horses, Texans pursued their enemy for miles, littering the prairie with the dead. Seven hundred thirty prisoners were rounded up. The rest were dead or wounded. Houston's losses were nine killed and 34 wounded.

The wily Santa Anna escaped on his horse, plunged into the bayou and did not reappear. The search squads rounded up all the escapees they could locate. The next day they dragged in one in dirty linen trousers, blue jacket and red cloth slippers whom they found hiding in the long grass. When Mexican prisoners spied him they murmured, *"El Presidente! El Presidente!"* Santa Anna asked to see General Houston.

He tried to run away as he was led before the big Texan who sat under a live oak tree with his injured leg propped up before him. The captive bowed, "I am General Antonio Lopez de Santa Anna, a prisoner of war, at your service."

"I am pleased to meet you. Sit down." Houston motioned to a nearby wooden chest.

Santa Anna asked for his interpreter, Colonel Almonte, who came forward. When the president broke down, he was given a dose of morphine. When he regained his composure he announced, "I wish to arrange for my immediate release."[3]

"How can you expect such treatment after your brutalities at the Alamo and Goliad?" Houston countered.

"Your men at the Alamo suffered the fate of the defeated in war," Santa Anna returned. "As for Goliad, I was ordered by my government to shoot every man found with a weapon in his hand."

"You are your government," retorted Houston. "A dictator has no superior."

"I have the order of Congress," the Mexican leader insisted. "And that compels me to treat as pirates all who are armed rebels."

Houston refused to yield, stating that he could make no terms, that such power belonged to the Texas Congress.

Santa Anna reminded the *Norteamericanos* that they now were offered the opportunity to be generous to the vanquished.

Whereupon Houston replied, "You should have thought of that at the Alamo."[4]

The Texans were in a turmoil, convinced that *El Presidente* should be executed *pronto*. Their commander in chief, however, although he was in intense pain with his wound, advocated restraint. He ordered Santa Anna's personal possessions restored to him and his luxurious marquee set up so that he might enjoy his usual comforts, while his conquerors stood guard.

El Presidente suggested that an armistice be declared but Houston pointed out that such action lay in the province of his government. The Mexican chief, standing his ground, replied that he did not like to deal with civilians. As a military man he was accustomed to make the decisions.

A treaty was drawn up in which Santa Anna promised to order all his troops to leave Texas. Hostilities were to cease and American prisoners were to be released. He pledged that he would work for the independence of the Texans and for a formal end of the conflict. The republic agreed to return him safely to Vera Cruz as soon as it was convenient.

Many of the Texans who had helped avenge the Alamo wanted Santa Anna shot but Sam Houston believed it wiser to send the general back to Mexico since he signed a treaty. The plan to convey him to Vera Cruz aroused opposition. It was decided to ship him temporarily to Orizaba, the country home of Dr. Orlando Phelps on the Brazos river. When the report reached Santa Anna that he might be executed by the Texans who mistrusted his promises, he was deeply disturbed and took poison to end his life. Dr. Phelps pumped out his stomach and saved him.

During his period of negotiation *El Presidente* was treated with consideration and permitted to pay a visit to President Andrew Jackson in Washington, D. C. He made some friends during his stay, charming people with his gracious manner.[5]

President Jackson sent the Mexican chief home to Vera Cruz aboard a United States navy frigate.

In the Treaty of San Jacinto Santa Anna had pledged that he would not again take up arms or aid in the war against Texan independence and he would "prepare the Mexican cabinet to receive a commission from Texas and Texas was not to extend beyond the Rio Grande."[6]

During his stay in Washington, D. C., Santa Anna appeared to have convinced President Andrew Jackson that he would be able to recover his place of leadership in Mexico and advance Jackson's proposal to sell Texas to the U.S.A.[7]

When Santa Anna returned to Vera Cruz after his defeat at San Jacinto, he was given a hostile welcome. United States Navy guards had to escort him to his home in Jalapa. He lost the election to the presidency to Bustamante but he was soon back in the limelight when the French bombarded Vera Cruz in an effort to collect debts that were owed her citizens. He was asked to defend the city. The French Admiral Baudin tried to kidnap Santa Anna who managed to escape in his undergarments. After organizing a resistance force, Santa Anna followed the French sailors to their boats. A small field gun was fired at him, killing his horse and shattering his leg.

This so-called "French Pastry War," because it started over a riot in a French restaurant, made the wounded champion a national hero. His amputated leg was placed in a mausoleum in Mexico City and he was again *El Presidente*. As soon as he assumed office he repudiated the agreements he made with the Texans and Andrew Jackson.[8]

The Hill household echoed with rejoicing as Asa and James Monroe returned from San Jacinto. The Fayette County men all came safely home. The surprise siesta attack against the resourceful Santa Anna demonstrated the ability of the new republic to cope with the arch schemer in Mexico City with his military might.

During the battle of San Jacinto James Monroe captured a young Mexican fifer boy, Joseph Mendes, who begged not to be sent back to Mexico. James Monroe took him home and the Hill family adopted him.

3

Another Summons

SIX YEARS OF RELATIVE PEACE had passed since San Jacinto. To better their condition the Hill family had moved from Gay Head to nearby Fayetteville in the same county. They built a new and larger home and the place was a beehive of activity with the extensive farm chores and the educational program of the children. Eight of them, plus Joseph Mendes, their adopted Mexican boy, had enrolled for the opening term in 1840 of Rutersville College, the first institution of higher learning in Texas.

The college was built in memory of the Reverend Martin Ruter, one of the first missionaries sent by the Methodist Church to Texas. The charter was granted by the republic with a donation of four leagues of land. Asa Hill was one of the original sponsors of the college.

Determined to train their children in the Christian faith, the Hills were loyal supporters of the Methodist Church which had the foresight to send its ministers to the new frontier of America. They embraced the teachings of John and Charles Wesley who stirred England in their efforts to alter the formalism and class distinction of the Church of England, speaking in the language of the people. They were reformers like the Pilgrims and Puritans before them.

The Reverend Hugh Kerr, great grandfather of George A. Hill Jr., published in New York in 1838 a book entitled *Poetic Description of Texas* in which he described the life of settlers and the conflict with Mexico:

> The land no previous culture had,
> Hence much privation was endur'd
> For want of bread-stuff, good or bad,
> And there it could not be procur'd.

> The only substitute at hand
> Was venison, when fully dried:
> With other meats at their command,
> Their daily meals were thus supplied.

> A few revolving seasons tend
> To change the scene—the farmer smiles—
> The culture of the fields extend
> And barns are stor'd with corn-piles.

> Domestic flocks and herds increase
> And poultry in the yards abound:
> This rural picture, still to trace,
> The garden fence is plac'd around.

> In that rude work-shop we may see
> A good supply of needful tools;
> The old man, busy as a bee,
> In mending ploughs or making stools.

> The good wife plies her needle fast;
> Young Sarah knitting by her side:
> Betty cooks the plain repast;

Small urchins on the watch-dog ride.
Brisk Mary has her last cut reel'd,
Which she throughout the day had spun:
The plough-boys enter, from the field,
Well pleas'd their daily task is done.

With basket light, and empty now,
The school-boys nimbly tripping home,
Approach with ceremonious bow,
All who meet them as they come.

The milk-supplying herd, at eve,
Come lowing o'er the spacious lawn:
The chopping axe is heard to cleave
The fuel for the next day-dawn.[1]

Thomas W. Bell, a young tutor at Rutersville College, wrote of the early days of the Texas Republic: "The tide of immigration poured in and was rapidly swelling her population. Where the buffalo and wild horse still roam and the nightly howl of the wolf and yells of the savage Indian might be heard, villages and towns were springing up as if by magic. Schools and churches arose in every part of the growing domain, spreading the light of knowledge to youth and inculcating the principles of gospel virtue to the population. Agriculture and commerce were flourishing."[2]

The Texans did not realize that Santa Anna had strapped on his $7,000 sword and was forming a new army of 6,000 men. As he planned his invasion of 1842 he stated that all captives would be executed and all supporters of rebellion would be treated as pirates.

On March 5, 1842, General Rafael Vazques, with 1,400 troops raided San Antonio de Bexar, cap-

The Hill School House as it looked in 1907. Building date unknown. (Courtesy Fayette County Record.)

tured considerable plunder and prisoners and scoot-
ed back across the border before the Texans could
organize. On September 11, 1842, General Adrian
Woll, with a force of 1,200, attacked San Antonio once
again. He sent a small boy with a white flag and prevailed on the Texans to surrender with the same old
story that they would be treated with all honor as
prisoners of war. Woll took away with him as captives a judge, a jury, clerks, lawyers and other citizens
when he was threatened with pursuit by Colonel
Matthew Caldwell and Captain Jack Hayes.

Shortly after Houston's appeal for volunteers a
Texas ranger visited the home of Asa Hill in Fayetteville. John Christopher Columbus was harvesting
corn in the field when he saw a trailing dust cloud
approaching from the west. He ran toward the barn
where Asa was rounding up the cows. The courier
did not dismount, pulling up to give the news that
another Santa Anna army was on its way to San
Antonio. Asa replied that he would start as soon as
possible. He would also check with his Fayetteville
neighbors and maybe take one of his boys.

As the big family gathered around the supper
table there was a hubbub of anxiety. Asa tried to calm
the troubled circle assuring them that the Texans
would soon drive the enemy south. The argument as
to who would accompany him continued over the
roast venison, hominy grits, turnip greens and corn
bread. All available hands were needed to bring in
the harvest. Green Washington would stay. Andrew
Jackson and James Monroe had done their part. Asa
Collingsworth was still young. Jeffrey Barksdale
could go this time.

John Christopher Columbus contended that he could ride as well as any man in Texas and could out-shoot most of them. Elizabeth Hill objected. He was too young. It was enough to send two members of her family. She recalled some of the hazards they had faced in the colony since leaving their home in Georgia. Their small settlement was far from shops. Supplies and clothing had to come from Houston. The days were full of labor, grinding meal, baking, making soap, cleaning milk pails, washing clothes in iron kettles over open fires, carding cotton and spinning. They were struggling to establish themselves and could ill afford another encounter with the Mexicans. She knew the price they had paid at the Alamo, Goliad and San Jacinto. Now another campaign was demanded. Certainly she should not be required to send three of hers, and John was a mere boy.

John pointed out that he was thirteen, going on to fourteen, and must go along to look after papa and Jeff. Not one of the Hills sensed at that moment that their little brother was to fulfill a major role in this historic expedition and prove instrumental in saving the lives of his father and brother and many other Texans.

In the babble of conversation John was not given an answer but he joined in preparations for the departure. There were rifles to clean, powder horns to fill, shot to be made ready, blankets to be located, buckskin trousers and jackets to mend and meat and bread prepared for the journey.

James Monroe was on the hearth of the fireplace cleaning and shining his rifle that had helped win the battle of San Jacinto. Now he was giving it to

Elizabeth Barksdale Hill, wife of Asa Hill.
(Hill family records.)

John to once again defend the Texans. Handing it to his young brother, he said, "Don't ever surrender it."

John held the gun firmly, answering, "I promise no Mexican will ever get it."

Mama was worried but she would let him go. It pleased her that he said he must go take care of his father and Jeffrey. "I must take it to the Lord in prayer," she said.

Preparations ended with bedtime. John crept out to the barn to check on his pony. The two had made the round trip alone to Austin, some 60 miles each way through wild country, to deliver their land deed to the court. He inspected his saddle and bridle and gave Jim Dandy a pat. He slipped back into the house and upstairs to bed.

The next morning Asa Hill and his two sons gathered at the village oak with the other volunteers. Under this same tree their neighbor, Mosby Dawson, had met with 16 Fayette men to set out for San Antonio. By October 25 about 1,200 had responded to Sam Houston's proclamation calling for a retaliatory raid on the Mexicans who had so long harassed the Texans.

The Hills and their group joined with other volunteers and assembled their horses and equipment near San Antonio. John made friends with other teenagers who had joined the expedition. Billie Reese, 15, was from Brazoria County. He had accompanied his brother, Charlie. Orlando Phelps, also from Brazoria, was the son of Dr. Orlando Phelps, who had entertained Santa Anna as his house prisoner after the defeat at San Jacinto, and saved his life when he tried to commit suicide by taking an overdose of morphine. There was Gilbert Brush of Fort Bend, and

Harvey Sellers of Fayette. John was the youngest of the boys, but due to his outgoing nature and winsome personality he was well liked by the men. Day after day he joined riders in exploring the countryside, hunting and speculating on how long it would be before they moved south after the Mexicans.

They were expected to forage for themselves. The boys were adept at hunting. They helped prepare roast venison over open fires and corn pone and black coffee. Evenings they would lie around the embers and listen to Asa Hill talk about the campaign that was slow in getting under way. Asa was a veteran, having served under General Andrew Jackson at the Battle of Horseshoe Bend in March, 1814.

Houston's volunteers had waited several weeks for the pursuit to begin. The impatient Texans rebuked their leaders for indecisiveness.

As Thomas J. Green, a member of the frustrated company, wrote in his diary: "Many of the men left their homes during the warm days of September, with pantaloons too thin for the sharp weather of November; and now, in the absence of a uniform military clothing establishment, they in the shortest time transferred the covering of many an unwary buck to their own legs. I never saw deer so plentiful. Many hundreds were killed, and the whole camp had more the appearance of a tremendous tanyard than an army which expected in a few days to meet the national enemy upon his own soil.[3]

"Indeed, the scene here presented was no bad illustration of the facility with which Texans can accommodate themselves to unforeseen emergencies; and he who could not creep upon the most keen-eyed buck, and 'ease him of his jacket,' was not fit for a soldier; and many who could not or would not do it, returned home, as they said, 'to get some warm clothing.'"[4]

The recruits who made up Houston's army were not all settlers. They came from many areas of the United States. They were touched by the appeal for support that came from the young republic and aroused by the atrocities of the Alamo and Goliad and by the treachery of Santa Anna, who violated his pledges made in 1836 by again raiding the republic. These men were foreigners to the story of Mexican-Texan relations that preceded 1842 and proved eager listeners to Hill and others who recounted for them the annals of continuing conflicts.

In spite of the desire to rid Texas once and for all from Santa Anna, there was confusion and dissent among members of the expedition. They had expected a speedy encounter with the bandits. Why did not the promised cannon arrive? Why had Sam Houston ordered them to proceed to the southwestern frontier, to concentrate their troops and enter enemy territory and then leave them to mark time near San Antonio?

First they waited for ammunition, then it was for artillery and then for a change of leaders. General Burleson had been popular with the men who were disappointed when he was replaced by General Alexander Somervell.

Amid the outrage over the capture of members of the Santa Fe expedition and the kidnapping of the San Antonio citizens, patriotic fervor ran high. Burleson was apparently ready to lead his volunteers south of the Rio Grande, but President Houston restrained him. When Somervell was placed at the head of the Texan forces he was ordered to proceed to the southwestern frontier to organize his men, and "If required to cross the Rio Grande."

There was time for discussion around the camp fires. Asa Hill, Captain Ewin Cameron, the Scottish highlander, Big Foot Wallace, the Virginia scout, and sturdy Thomas Jefferson Green spoke their minds.

Reports reached them about the tragedy that befell Captain Nicholas Mosby Dawson's company which had grown to 53 as they had moved on foot from La Grange to San Antonio. They were attacked near Salado Creek by 400 Mexican cavalrymen and after a valiant defense raised the white flag. The Mexicans charged and lanced and hacked to pieces with their swords many who survived the rounds of combat. Thirty-five lay dead on the field, 15 were taken prisoner and three escaped. The prisoners were led to General Woll, who assured them they would be treated as prisoners of war. They were marched to Mexico and imprisoned in Perote Castle. The dead were stripped of their clothing and left on the ground to be devoured by wolves and birds of the air.[5]

Colonel Caldwell's detail discovered their naked bodies, so mutilated by cannon shot, sabre and lance wounds as to be unrecognizable. The heads of a number of them were nearly severed. The cold rain had washed them of blood and given them a ghostly appearance.

This additional perfidy enraged the Texan volunteers.

The men asked, was their effort to prove another Alamo, another Goliad, another Salado

Creek? Due to lack of support and leadership were they to fall into some new trap and be wiped out?[6]

John Hill listened to these discussions and observed amid the complaining that volunteers kept slipping away every day, announcing that they were going home to fetch a better horse, a new gun or some winter clothing.

Big Foot (William) Wallace had set out from Virginia for Texas when word was received that his brother Sam had been murdered in the Goliad massacre. A giant in size and strength at the age of 23, he built himself a cabin near La Grange, not far from the Hills. He heard of Jack Hays and the Texas Rangers, made his way to San Antonio and became a ranger. When General Woll staged his raid, Big Foot urged pursuit by the volunteers who had gathered. He rebelled against General Somervell's delay. John Hill liked this carefree extrovert who hailed from his own country, and the two were soon close friends. Big Foot was for action and found ways to enliven the dull hours of waiting.

After days of stalling and grousing it was announced that the army would move south in late November toward the Neuces River and the destination of Laredo, some 153 miles away. Keyed up by the report that they would soon see action, John Hill lay wrapped in his blankets on the earth between Asa and Jeff as the camp fires shrank from glowing flames to black nothingness and the night wind ran waves through the dry grass.

He heard the click-clank of a bell worn by the leader of the pack mules as the animals grazed.

Many had gone home due to the threat of

approaching winter and the unrest. There was no discipline as in a regular army. Men were free to come and go as they chose, to hunt deer and make buckskin trousers and jackets with which to face the coming cold. John rode every day with the mounted hunters, bringing in his share of venison. After the hunt he helped skin the deer, salt the hides for tanning and sew the buckskin into clothing. They were crude pants and coats but they were warm and better than the clothes they brought with them, which had become dirty and ragged.[7]

One wonders why Mexico did not send her people to develop Texas instead of asking the Yankees to do the job. They had thousands of peons, ignorant and impoverished, who needed economic opportunity. Evidently their wealthy rulers wanted the initiative and skills of their northern neighbors to develop and enrich the land for them.

4

Impatient Volunteers

$\mathcal{A}$S THEY SET OUT TOWARD LAREDO there was no fife or drum, just a dull, long march on rolling table-land studded at intervals with clumps of live oaks, post oaks and muskeet. John was part of the moving column of some 700 riders, 1,200 horses and mules and 500 cattle. He jogged beside Jeffrey, reins held tensely, rifle alert and ready as if expecting a sudden encounter with the Mexican cavalry. He watched Jeff, who rode loose-jointed, at ease, rolling in his saddle, a gangling towhead.[1]

The procession halted as its leaders debated the course they should take to Laredo. Someone announced that they were not following the Presidio Trail, the one along which the San Antonio prisoners had taken after their recent capture. It was the established route. Why should they follow the Laredo Trail which was wild and difficult? But under Somervell's orders they stuck to the rougher course.

The whole country was a wilderness, "covered thick with chapparal and presenting an appearance more dismal than anything I ever beheld. The water was often brackish and the only foliage we could get for our horses was the mesquite grass, which as it was the dead of winter, was very dry and afforded them but slight sustenance."[2]

When they reached the Neuces River on December 4 it was a raging torrent. Someone announced that they would have to camp here till the water went down.

"Camp nothing!" cried Captain Cameron. "We will bridge the stream."[3] Cameron and Big Foot Wallace plunged their horses into the chill water and swam across. Captain Jack Hayes, the Texas ranger, told the men to build a bridge. The captain had been appointed by Sam Houston to form a company of scouts to keep watch on the Mexicans and Indians. He was the founder of the rangers.

Tugging axes from their saddlebags, they chopped at the base of tall trees and felled them so that they rested across the river. The ingenious rangers constructed a crude bridge of tree trunks and branches and the men were able to cross over the stream. They dismounted and struggled to lead their horses and mules through the mucky land. In two days' time they moved forward only five miles. Sometimes the sod in the post oak bog would hold a man but break under the weight of an animal. Jim Dandy was bogged in the mud with a hopeless look on his usually cheery face. John and Jeff tugged to free him.

Big Foot Wallace slapped the flanks of his gargantuan mule that puffed through dilated nostrils while others pushed on his rump and tugged at his head. There were shouts of laughter as the great beast was pulled to firmer ground. Most of the men joined in the widespread grumbling: Why hadn't "Slow

Poke" Somervell taken the other trail to Laredo?

William Preston Stapp, a member of the expedition, wrote of this ordeal:

"The line stretched about a mile in length and coiling into the most fantastic curves: men, mules and horses, half submerged and all floundering as though possessed by a general nightmare, produced a spectacle of the most ludicrous aspect imaginable. It was not until near the close of a cold and drizzling day allotted us for this queer navigation, that we effected a landing. Many of our pack mules stuck fast in the bog, and finding it impractical to leave them, they were promptly shot to preserve them against the slow and lingering death that awaited them."[4]

Another Texan described the post oak bog; horses were "down upon the grass, their legs entirely out of sight, and their noses upon the ground in perfect quietude, as well as to say to their owners, 'You put me here, now get me out.'"

The encounter came to an end and the men at length reached firm ground. The animals were happy to graze the long grass and the ripe bean pods on the mesquite. The spirits of the troops revived somewhat over their fires built of twigs that soon set coffee pots boiling and meat sizzling. After the evening meal John and his small company spied Lieutenant Daniel Drake Henrie, who had developed into a popular entertainer. He had been around the world and spoke several languages. Evenings he would stage his one-man vaudeville show around the camp fire.[5]

The jovial chap from Brazoria was urged to speak a piece for them. Lieutenant Dan bowed low, sweeping his hands in front of his mud-spattered boots. Assuming a heroic stance, he declaimed with melodramatic gestures:

> Half a league, half a league,
> Half a league onward,
> All in the Valley of Death
> Rode the six hundred.
> Forward, the Light Brigade!
> "Charge for the guns," he said.
> Into the Valley of Death
> Rode the six hundred.[6]

Then one of the men pulled from his pocket a newly published booklet of poems by Hugh Kerr, his Fayetteville neighbor, and read one about their present conflict with Santa Anna:

> Mexico, to curb that rising infant state,
> Her abject convicts there did send,
> And many garrisons create
> Her hostile purpose to extend.
>
> The settlers were by law exempt,
> A stated time, from import dues:
> That law was treated with contempt,
> Evincing their tyrannic views.
>
> And men were station'd at the ports,
> With military aid at hand,
> Exacting duties on imports
> Before they would permit to land.
>
> Collusion then, and bribery,
> Were there commenc'd in Spanish style;
> A system fraught with perjury,
> Chicanery, and sordid guile.

Regardless of all civil rights,
Despotic mandates were sent forth
By military upstart wights,
Announcing vengeance in their wrath

Against all such as dar'd to speak
In opposition to their will;
Nor waited long for cause to seek;
Tyrannic threats they soon fulfil.

At Anuauc, respected men,
Were basely chain'd—the felon's lot;
And very briefly sentenc'd them,
Like malefactors, to be shot.

But Texas freemen could not brook
The savage conduct of those men;
And hence they promptly undertook
And forced them to retire again.[7]

Big Foot Wallace spread the news that two Mexican scouts had been captured. One escaped and the other was placed under his watch care. He slept with the prisoner so that he could not possibly escape. The wily scout, however, outwitted the ranger. He slipped a saddle into his place under the blankets and stole away in the darkness of the night. Big Foot was chagrined and the camp was alarmed. There was now no chance of surprise. The enemy would be warned and on their guard.

Nevertheless they set out the next morning for Laredo. The march that should have been made in a week took 17 days. On December 7 they were close enough to make their move and planned to attack at dawn. Late that night Big Foot Wallace and the

rangers led an advance into the city. Cautiously enter-
ing the stronghold of the pursued, they were shocked
to meet no resistance. Not a soldier was in sight. They
had beat a safe retreat south into Mexico. The townspeople, warned by the military, greeted their invaders
with Latin diplomacy, "Good day, American visitors.
We welcome you."

"This proved an irritating loss to our men, as
many of them were dismounted, their horses having
given out on the way, and the wearied riders being
compelled to long marches, packing their baggage
and provisions on their shoulders. Many of them
labored under the additional inconvenience of having
lost their blankets and clothes; and as the winter had
set in with unusual severity, the absence of such
indispensable comforts was keenly felt. Added to
this, our last day's provisions were expended, and
not withstanding the voluntary bankruptcy of the
town, the general found it necessary to lay a requisition on its authorities for supplies."[8]

Morale was at low ebb as William P. Stapp recorded in his journal: "Murmurs and discontent were
openly and loudly expressed at this retrograde movement, and General Somervell indignantly charged
with the pusillanimous intent of an ignominious
return home, without pulling a trigger on the enemy.
His capacity for command, and his courage and con-
tent in the affair at hand, were fully criticized and
contemptuously denounced by men and officers,
almost within his hearing. Venting their displeasure
in mutinous threats and imprecations, the march was
continued through impenetrable thickets until eight
o'clock P.M., when we halted for the night in the chap-

paral, without forage for our horses, or water for ourselves. Here was another pretext for complaint, which furnished the most fruitful abuse of general and officers; which can only be truly appreciated by those who are familiar with the unbridled tongues of a volunteer camp."[9]

Amid the grousing General Somervell made an address and requested that "all who felt desirous of prosecuting the war and penetrating into Mexican territory were requested to retire on a neighboring hill. Near 500 volunteers responded to his call. It was next announced that such as were anxious to return home were at liberty to go and this unwarlike privilege was immediately asserted by 150 of the drafted men under Colonel Bennett."

A council of the officers of the volunteer force was held and it was resolved to descend the Brazos, capture Guerero and continue the descent to Mier and Camargo, unless intercepted and repulsed by a superior force. The men moved out to hunt for food. In addition to droves of mustangs and wild cattle that roamed the country there were deer, elk, turkeys and Mexican hogs.

Continuing the march south for three days through bogs and thickets, the expedition struck the Brazos some six miles above Guerero. The Brazos River was a swift and majestic stream, but at this season its waters were low and it was only 300 yards in width. Securing a few small boats, the company proceeded to embark for the opposite side. By three P.M. some 200 had reached the south bank when General Green and Captain Bogart who had gone ahead toward the town with a small force, came hurrying back pursued by the Mexican General Canales with 200 cavalrymen. The Texans formed ranks and waited but the enemy galloped away.[10]

The next morning the balance of the troops crossed over and started the march into town. They were met by the *alcalde*, who formally surrendered the place, promising that he would comply with the request to furnish provisions for the Texans. He entreated the commander to spare his citizens the terror of a visit by his men. The Texans concurred, providing the town would deliver 500 beeves and $5,000.

When the Texans returned to claim the supplies, a "few mules caparisoned with tattered saddle blankets" and $173 was all they could collect. The villagers announced that the rancheros had driven the livestock from their community.[11]

A report had reached Somervell that General Pedro Ampudia was advancing from the south at the head of a large Mexican force. Whether unduly apprehensive or utterly disgusted with the disorganization and dissatisfaction that prevailed, Somervell, with about 100 followers, determined to relinquish all further operations on the frontier and retrace his steps to Texas. "Except with a limited number of his personal friends and adherents the general had become odious to men and officers, and most of those who resolved to accompany him back, cordially sympathized in the contempt and distrust so universally meted out to him."[12]

Asa Hill and his sons shared the antipathy toward Somervell that was expressed by their comrade in the expedition, William P. Stapp, along with other aggressive men like Thomas Jefferson Green,

William S. Fisher, Big Foot Wallace and Ewin Cameron.

General Somervell was disgruntled by the move into Mexico. He gave an order to cross back to the shore of Texas and then burn the Mexican boats they found on the river so the enemy could not follow them. Tom Green protested and suggested that they hide the boats in the woods below. Volunteers carried out this secret maneuver. Captains Cameron, Eastland and Pearson were supported by the Hills and others who wanted to carry the expedition into Mexico.

The men were disheartened and hungry. The *alcalde* had tricked them. No beeves had shown up, no blankets had been delivered. The Mexicans had robbed them many times. Why shouldn't they cross over and seize what they needed? Others, however, reasoned, we have been away long enough. It is time to quit.

General Somervell shouted, "Order, men. Silence! We can spend all winter arguing. Without support we cannot win. All who wish to march north with me, step forward ten paces. We will leave at once."[13]

Two hundred men moved ahead out of line, murmuring that Sam Houston had let them down; they could not fight without supplies. Three hundred and three stood firm.

The 303 met to reorganize. William S. Fisher was elected colonel. He was a native of Virginia who had come to Texas in 1834. He had served in the Federal War with the Mexican forces under General Canales and knew the language and the country. Fisher had warned a year before that Santa Anna was planning to invade Texas.[14]

General Thomas Jefferson Green.
(Courtesy Texas State Library.)

Thomas Jefferson Green was made second officer and commander of the boats that were to be used to move down the Rio Grande.

The courage of Asa Hill and the 303 around him must have wavered as they saw good friends leave on the homeward journey. They tried to reassure one another that they had taken the right stand and that with their aggressive leaders and a select group of dedicated volunteers they would avenge the wrongs that had been perpetrated upon their people.

John and Jeffrey took their stand along with their youthful friends among those who were determined to see it through.

5

Impending Encounter

$\mathcal{F}$ISHER AND GREEN HAD EXPLAINED to their company of 303, "It is our mission to enter Mexico and
liberate our fellow citizens who have been taken captive. We intend to do battle with any Mexican force
we meet. We go as representatives of the Republic of
Texas and under its flag, but we must provide our
own supplies and munitions. We will make levies on
the towns, demanding provisions and blankets and
when this fails we will forage for ourselves."

Seven captains were chosen, including Ewin
Cameron, Charles Reese and William Eastland. John
Hill and the teenagers were on hand December 20 as
Tom Green organized his navy and were assigned as
marines under Samuel C. Lyons, an old sailor, who
had been made sailing master. Sam was master of the
flag ship which carried a red flag at its mast. There
were six large barges in the flotilla, capable of carrying about 125 men per vessel and several smaller
boats. Each one had its commander and crew. Their
mission was to transport the men down the Rio
Grande, destroy enemy craft that they found, carry
troops to the Mexican side and, if necessary, be ready

in time of retreat to ferry them back to Texas soil.[1]

With the spy company under Big Foot Wallace in advance, the force set sail under the lone star flag of the republic. The river at this point was a broad and deep stream averaging 1,200 yards in width, flowing between high bluffs on the Mexican side and fertile fields on the north.

December 23 they pitched camp farther south on the Rio Grande on the east bank about seven miles from the Mexican town of Mier. Spies had slipped into Mier After talking with the *alcalde* and some Americans, they learned that General Canales had just evacuated the place, but that other troops were expected at any hour. Following a council of war it was decided to march into Mier and demand supplies. Next morning Colonel Fisher spoke to the troops who had crossed the river with him: "You are upon an honorable service, not one of pillage; your country will look to you for a soldier-like discharge of this service."

As they entered Mier the *alcalde* and the principal men invited Fisher and Green to the city hall where they asked for a list of what was needed by the Texans.

General Green wrote out the requisition:

"All government stores of every kind, including cannon, small fire arms, powder, lead, munitions of war of every kind, tobacco. Five days rations for 1,200 men: 40 sacks of flour, 1,200 pounds of sugar, 600 pounds of coffee, 200 pairs of strong boots, 100 pairs of pantaloons, 100 blankets."[2]

"I have to do this for the Mexican army," the *alcalde* assented, "and I can expect no less in dealing with you."

The magistrate called upon the citizens to get busy collecting the items listed on the requisition.

"The materials are being brought in," he explained, "but we have no wagons or teams available to deliver them this evening. It is already late and growing dark."

"Your promise is not enough, Mr. *Alcalde*," said Fisher. "We must take you with us as a hostage with the understanding that the supplies will be at the river opposite our camp the first thing in the morning!"

Ordered to mount his horse, the *alcalde* drooped in a forlorn manner, moaning to himself as the guard escorted him out of Mier. When they reached the river he burst into an impassioned pleas: "I wish to return at this time to Mier. The commanding general will come back at any moment. It is imperative that I be there to communicate with him."

"Sorry," said Fisher firmly. "You must stay with us."

John rode out on Jim Dandy with others to meet the officers as they led the dignitary from the river toward camp, staring at the colorful costume of the *alcalde* who carried a silver-headed cane to which was attached a bunch of silk tassels, symbol of authority.

John and the other boy troopers had suggested that the next *alcalde* should be brought into camp and forced to deliver the promised supplies. Their elders had dubbed them the "fire eaters." Their idea had been adopted. General Green commented, "If I had a company like these lads, I could conquer Mexico."

It was a rough climb from the river side where their boats were moored to the camp on the hill. In the movement toward the encampment a rifle shot shocked the tenseness. Young Chris Yocum collapsed on the ground.[3]

One of the men crept back from the forward line "My God! It was *my* gun. Struck a mesquite bush and it went off!"

The camp was strangely still in spite of the excitement caused by the presence of the prisoner. The *alcalde* was out of place in his regalia among the ragged Texans with their shaggy hair and beards. Their buckskin and homespun trousers and jackets were torn and dirty. They shared a spartan supper with the magistrate—a few slabs of beef. Those who spoke Spanish tried to draw him out, but he was frightened and cautious.[4]

The *alcalde* was touched by the sadness of the fire eaters; John, Billie Reese, Orlando Phelps, Harvey Sellars and Gilbert Brush, and followed them to look down solemnly on the body now wrapped in a ragged blanket. "Poor little fellow," he murmured, "so innocent, so far from his home."

The men gathered around the grave they had dug. The service from the *Book of Common Prayer* was read by Chaplain Fontaine and the boy's body lowered. When the grave had been filled they laid rocks on it to ward off coyotes. There was no volley because ammunition was short.

The day before Christmas dawned cold and bleak. The *alcalde* looked wretched as he staggered to his feet. "The requisition will doubtless come at any time," he kept repeating. He had expected to be treated with respect by the Texans and at least be offered a tent in which to rest, but he discovered that the Texans flung themselves on the ground with not enough cover to keep a poor *peon* warm. Tom Green, who took the *alcalde* under custody, forced him to sleep with him under the same blanket, compelling the Mexican dignitary to place one leg between his own so he could guarantee his presence through the night.

The Texans turned their backs on the camp and the stony grave of young Yocum and moved along the river with its high banks. They had agreed to assemble at the mouth of El Centro, a small stream that emptied into the Rio Grande, a short distance below the camp. The town of Mier was located some three miles away on its southern bank. They waited for the arrival of the cattle the *alcalde* had promised but not one appeared. The day was passed in hunger and anxiety. Unnerved by the threatening of his captors, the *alcalde* was ushered to bed supperless, again the unwilling bedfellow of General Green.

Christmas morning Captain Baker's spies captured a Mexican who reported that General Pedro de Ampudia had occupied Mier and had seized the supplies that were to be sent to the Texans. There was no breakfast and no chance for food.

"General Ampudia has occupied Mier," word flew through the camp.

"General Canales is with him. They have several hundred men and two cannon."

"They have commandeered the food that should have come to us."

The spies had brought reports on Mier. It was a community of 8,000 people about six miles from the Rio Grande River in the State of Tamaulipas, the largest and richest town upon the river next to Matamoras. The river curved about, passing to the north side and flowing southeast, into the Rio Grande. The river banks were steep and wooded. The scouts soon discovered that there were two well-known fording places in the river. After careful thought they chose El Cantaro.[5]

Mier had been founded in 1753 in honor of señor Don Josè Sernando Teriza de Mier D.D., the delegate to the Spanish *Cortes* from this area. Blanket weaving was the chief industry and almost every home was equipped with a primitive loom for weaving wool. The town was laid out in typical Spanish style around an open plaza. The church and the residence of the general were on the west side. The *alcalde*'s office was located on the east side next to the government warehouses. In this square the townspeople gathered for daytime markets, evening visiting and religious festivals.

The captains briefed their men on what they might face in the battle for Mier. It was voted to cross over and fight. A guard of 30 was left in charge of the horses and supplies. John and his fellow marines ferried the forces over the Rio Grande.

By four P.M. they succeeded in transporting their troops to the opposite shore. Throwing out advance columns, they moved forward to the town some three miles distant.[6]

Suddenly they heard the report of the first encounter with the Mexican cavalry. The spies had bumped into a unit of mounted men who bore down on them. Big Foot shouted, "Run, or they'll get you."

The Mexicans charged with lowered lances. After a sharp hand-to-hand struggle, the Texans jumped from their horses and took to their heels. One ranger broke through to call for help. "The Mexicans grabbed my legs," he yelled, "as I was climbing over a pole fence. My boots slipped off in their hands and I got away. Sam Walker was pounced on and hog tied. They caught four others."

As darkness closed in the Texans occupied a high bluff on the river which they prepared to ford in order to reach Mier. Scouts had determined to make a try at the El Cantaro ford, leading the *alcalde* to the banks of the stream and demanding that he show them the safest crossing. The river bed was full of jagged rocks and deep water holes. El Cantaro ford was a strip of pebbly bottom 60 yards wide in the midst of swift moving waters. Captain Reese was sent across first to locate the enemy pickets.

At that moment the captured Sam Walker was standing before Pedro de Ampudia. "Tell me how many Texans are there in your force and what are your plans?" the general demanded. "I warn you that if you report falsely to me you will be executed."[7]

"I realize that I am your prisoner," Walker replied coolly, "and that my life is in your hands. But may I remind you that it is not the habit or nationality of Texans to lie."

"How many troops have you?"

"Three hundred and three."

"That sounds dubious to me. It is incredible that you would venture into Mexico with such a handful."

"Well, that's all there are. We had more, but they got tired waiting for a fight and went home."

"With that small number you would not have the audacity to attack."

"You need have no doubt, general," Sam retorted. "You don't know the Texans. They would pursue and attack you in hell!"[8]

While General Ampudia received this news from the ranger, the Texans were moving forward cautiously in the rain.

"Guard your guns while crossing."

"Keep your powder dry."

"The pickets may fire. Make the *alcalde* march in front."

The magistrate was shaken by the rifle fire and pleaded, "I have done all in my power to help you. You ought not to carry me into battle. I have a beloved wife and children at home!"

One member of the expedition wrote of that Christmas night:

"The evening was gloomy and wet, the rain driving furiously in our faces, while the gathering obscurity of approaching night, falling upon the wild and naked hills through which we marched, seemed ominous of the ill-starred fortunes awaiting us. At a distance of a mile from the river we fell in with some unmounted look-outs of the enemy who fled with the utmost precipitation the moment we came into view. Further on our advance came up with their outposts and drove them in, one after another, until we reached the northern bank of the river, a few hundred yards from the village. When we arrived here it was nine o'clock at night and unusually dark.

"Amid the darkness and showers of musket balls, our gallant little band waded the river opposite the town, guided in the passage by the ceaseless blaze of the evening's musketry. Captain Baker's company who were stationed a short distance below our point of crossing, succeeded in a slight measure in diverting their force, but not a gun was discharged from our party before we reached the beach under the brow of the village. General Green, with a picked company of volunteers, led the advance, the imploring and shuddering *alcalde* enclosed in the forward platoon, begging in low and plaintive tones to be allowed to fall back to the rear.[9]

General Green had chosen a spot protected by the small river embankment to place some of the scouts and boatmen to open fire on the cavalry above them on the hill of Mier in an effort to deceive the enemy. He initiated the barrage with nine shots from his repeating rifle. The company kept up the fire while Green crept downstream to supervise fording.

John slid along the treacherous bank. He clung to the brush to keep from tumbling into those below. He plunged in waist deep to wade the icy stream, holding his rifle and blanket roll high.

The rushing of the river tended to drown the noise of their crossing. John hurried on to join his company that was pressing toward Mier. General Green was in charge of the right wing, which included Asa, Jeff and the fire eaters. They stumbled into a group of Mexican pickets who were not expecting them.

"*Quien viva?*" the pickets cried. "Let them have it, boys!" was the answer.

About a hundred shots were poured into them. Not a rifle spoke back. The Texans could hear the bellowing of a Mexican colonel to his troops a few hundred yards away, "Charge them, cavalry!" But the horsemen refused to stir.

At this point the *alcalde* took advantage of the confusion, slipped into the darkness and disappeared. Sammy Lyons, sailing master, who was in charge of the magistrate, opened fire under the excitement with his double barreled Joe Manton, forgetting the hostage under his charge.

"Where is the *alcalde*?" cried General Green. "By my soul, general, he is adrift!" answered the chagrined old sailor.

The enemy pickets retreated as the Texans drove them into Mier.

6

A Daring Venture

*T*HE MEXICANS HAD PLACED THEIR CANNON at two corners of the plaza to protect the streets that led from the east. The Texans crept in at the northeast. As the right wing reached the square the artillery opened fire with grape and cannister.

"Under cover!" was the command. "Let them fire, then jump out and shoot while they reload."

Using this strategy and dodging the cannon balls under cover of walls and alleyways, the sharp shooting Texans picked off the gunners and pushed ahead to take shelter in the houses on the plaza. The public square covered an acre or more. It was formed of parallel rows of stone structures, intersected at each angle by streets that spread into the town. At the northeast and northwest debouches there were two six-pound guns, while the houses and the square itself were filled with Mexican troops and a strong reserve was stationed beyond the western walls.

The left wing was under fire from the Mexicans' blunderbusses that blazed away from the housetops. A Britisher, who had volunteered to help in the war of independence and who was admired because of the neatness and decorum of his dress, was struck by lead from one of these guns. Mexicans seized his body and began stripping off his clothing. The Texans fought to drive them off, shooting down twenty men.[1]

"Take possession of that row of buildings!" Green ordered.

Under shelter they set to work to dry their powder and get their rifles in shape. The guns had been dampened by the rain and the river crossing. The men crowded into the welcome refuge and took stock of their position.

Had it not been for the darkness and their unfamiliarity with the Mexican defenses, they might have fought to take the square and clean out the enemy that night. Wishing to conserve ammunition, they decided to cease firing until daylight. The sturdy walls afforded them defense, and they set to work to plan their strategy.

The townspeople had abandoned the square early in the day, rushing off into the woods with their valuables, but fortunately they left a supply of jerked beef, fresh bread and jars of water which helped check the hunger of the newcomers. As the rain ceased and the moon appeared they could see the plaza clearly with preparations being made on the roof tops, barricades being erected in the streets and cavalry dashing about.

The dwellings were built one against another, forming continuous walls with partitions between. The sections they occupied were one story high with tall grated windows that fronted each other at the terminus of an avenue that led to the great square. The left wing, under Captains Reese and Pearson, entered the row of buildings on the opposite side of the plaza. Captain Cameron took up a position with his men in a house that was surrounded by a stone wall.

After the outer doors had been crashed by Green's men he gave the order to smash an opening into the partition and work forward toward the battery. They found a crowbar and a log to batter their way through and open a line of communication. They then fell into fitful sleep while the guard kept watch.

With the first rays of dawn the Mexicans trained their six pounders upon the Texan quarters while showers of musket balls crashed against the stone and mortar.

"They are breaking openings for us," a Texan cried "Man those breeches!" came the order. "Pick them off with your rifles!"

"They're shooting from the portholes on the left wing. We have them under crossfire."

"Captain Reese and Captain Pearson will make it hot for them from that side."

The men broke through the inner partitions until they were within some fifty yards of the battery.

"Come on, boys," General Green called. "This is the place for you fire eaters. That battery of theirs is making too much noise. It is your job to stop it. It might hurt somebody by accident."

John squeezed in behind the breached wall beside Orlando Phelps, Billie Reese, Harvey Sellers and Gilbert Brush. The fire eaters were under fire.[2]

"Whenever a Mexican tries to load a cannon, take careful aim and hit him in the head. Fire one at time, keep at it until ordered to stop." The general hurried off to arrange the defenses.

John looked down the sight of his rifle and pulled the trigger, catching an artilleryman in the temple.

The fire eaters sighted through their openings, aimed, fired and reloaded. John kept track of the number by shot, seventeen, all in the forehead. It was a tense game under the stench of rifle smoke, the thunder of explosions and the shrieks of the wounded.

The cannons were manned at dawn by a full company of artillerymen. By nine o'clock the cannonading was silenced. Fifty-five gunners were dead and five disabled due to the skillful aim of the boys and other Texans. Captain Castro was the only officer of the artillery corps still in action.

The big guns were abandoned. Mexican troops still fired from the tops of the plaza edifices. Whenever a Mexican head was raised for a moment of reconnaissance above the parapets on the housetops, a Texan bullet found its mark. The stone spouts that projected from the gutters dripped with blood. Holes were broken in the roof by Fisher's men who fired until they cleared all houses within range.

Word was passed to the fire eaters that Jeffrey Hill had been shot. Clutching his rifle, John made his way through the break in the partition in search of Dr Brennen. He found him bending over Jeffrey who was laid on the floor on a blanket. The doctor told him that his brother had received a rifle wound in the chest and was suffering shock from the musket fire. John turned back heavy-hearted to his post of duty.

Inspired by the antics of the cavalry, a Mexican column charged down the street to the north of the building where Green's men were quartered. Colonel Fisher and twenty others ran out to repulse them. Several were wounded in the heavy firing, including Fisher, whose right thumb was shot off.

Meanwhile word flashed that Fisher had been injured. Green rushed to check on his condition. Fisher was vomiting from the shock of the gunshot injury. Captain Cameron was in trouble also. His wounded had been carried into the building inside the courtyard while he and his men fired from behind the stone wall. Under pressure of attack, Cameron, two hundred pounds of muscle, in his tartan plaid with bowie knife at his belt, tirelessly wielded his huge rifle that fired ten balls to the pound.

But the Scot was worried about the shooting from the housetops near the church. During a lull he ordered his men to collect stones from the wall and yard in case they ran out of ammunition.

After the charge on Colonel Fisher another force bore down upon Cameron. The Texans had to stand unprotected to shoot into the wave of attackers and were also exposed to fire from the roof. They delivered a heavy volley and the first rank of Mexicans who went down were hidden by a screen of smoke. With rifles empty they faced the second wave.

"Boys, to your stones!" shouted Captain Cameron.

The Texans grabbed the rocks they had harvested as a precaution and hurled them. The well aimed missiles smashed skulls and felled some assailants. The balance, surprised by the weird defense of their foes, broke and ran.

But Cameron now had three dead and seven

wounded. One-fifth of his men were eliminated. "Keep your heads down," he yelled. "I'll run for aid."

He found Fisher weak and violently nauseated. "I need help, sir," he announced.

The commander was too severely shaken to answer. Cameron's bad news set everyone shouting in confusion and offering suggestions. Panic threatened.

General Green leaped upon a table. "Silence!" he called. "Give aid to Cameron, you there and you. Back to your posts, men!"

Green's plain words put the Texans on their mettle again. And then, unexpectedly, Dr. Sinnickson, who had been captured by the Mexicans as the Texans tried to enter Mier, appeared in the plaza marching toward them with a white flag in his hand.

The fire eaters raised their rifles, guessing that the enemy was sending Doc to announce that they were ready to surrender. From their vantage point it appeared to be their victory.

Dr. Sinnickson, after his capture, had been led before General Ampudia for questioning. He was unfamiliar with the state of the battle. If he had known the carnage the Mexicans were suffering he might have saved the day. For at that moment General Ampudia's and his officers' horses were saddled and waiting to carry the Mexican force away from the bloody battle in Mier. The gate of the church yard was open toward Matamoros road and preparations were being made for a getaway.

The canny Mexicans suggested as a last stroke of strategy that they might try the "white flag trick" and possibly bluff the Texans into surrender.

Since Dr. Sinnickson had been captured he was not conscious of the losses the Mexicans had met. He had not been able to talk with other American prisoners. The surgeon general on Ampudia's staff spotted Sinnickson and suggested to Canales and Carasco that Sinnickson might be employed in this deceptive move. The unwitting Texas doctor was considered a good prospect for the act with the white flag.

"How many men do you Texans have?" General Ampudia asked Dr. Sinnickson.

"Three hundred and three in all but not all in action here."

"They put up a fierce fight for so small a number. How many have you in killed and wounded?"

"That I do not know. I have not been with the main force in Mier."

"Who is your commanding officer?"

"Colonel William S. Fisher."

"I order you to bear a flag of truce to Colonel Fisher," Ampudia stated, "and demand an immediate surrender."[3]

Sinnickson stood silent, not believing his ears and unwilling to take part in any betrayal of his own men.

General Ampudia said sharply, "It is useless for you to refuse. You will be compelled to do as I order. He seized the doctor by the shoulder. "Do you understand?"

Colonel Carasco took hold of the other shoulder and shook him. Without waiting for an answer, Genera Canales and other officers thrust him out into the plaza, jabbed a white flag into his hand and insisted "Go or you will be shot!"

As Dr. Sinnickson advanced from the east with his white flag, a company of Mexican infantry crept in from the west along the edge of the plaza under cover of the truce move.

"A white flag and advancing troops! It looks like fake deal!" Green snapped. He noted that the weapons of the enemy were not reversed but were in a hostile attitude. "You take that first man," he ordered the Texan next to him. The man fired and one of the Mexican troops fell.[4]

"I'll take the next two," Green opened with his repeating rifle with good success. The rest of the infantry dodged around the corner of a building.

General Green did not realize that those were to be the last three shots fired in the battle of Mier.

Meanwhile, Dr. Sinnickson stood before Colonel Fisher. "Cease firing," Fisher ordered.

Fisher looked intently at the Mexican officers who were following the doctor. "What is the meaning of the white flag? Are they asking terms?"

"No, Colonel," Sinnickson replied. "They have forced me to come with the demand for our surrender."

"Surrender?" murmured Fisher, who was in agony with his pain, looking at the ground, revolver clutched in his uninjured hand.

"This is what Ampudia has demanded that I carry to you," the doctor added. "'Tell Colonel Fisher that he must surrender with his whole force in five minutes or I will cause them all to be put to the sword and give no quarter. To accomplish this I have 1,700 regular troops and look every moment for a reinforcement of 800. If he will cause his troops to lay down their arms and surrender, their lives shall be spared and they shall be treated with all the humanity and deference due them as prisoners of war; and furthermore I will exercise my influence with the supreme government to prevent their being marched to the City of Mexico and will have them retained east of the mountains until they are released or exchanged.'" The doctor shook his head sadly as he rehearsed the terms.

"We thought it was the enemy that was asking for terms!" cried General Green.

"We have beaten them," said Cameron.

The Texans had realized with the dawn that they were facing overwhelming odds in confronting the larger enemy forces, but they had determined to continue their assault.

Their offensive so startled Ampudia, as he saw his men murdered, that he had planned a retreat in case his white flag strategy failed. He was almost ready to leave Mier to the Texans.

As the report ran like wildfire through the Texans, they cried, "We will never surrender our arms!"

A group of Mexican officers, following in the wake of the white flag, slipped into the ranks of their enemy. "Watch out," General Green warned, "these men are spies." Those who had entered the company of the Texans were high officers—General De La Vega, Colonels Carasco and Blanco and Padre de Lire, the priest from Camargo. Several of them had known Fisher when he served with the Mexican army in the Federal War. "Greetings, good friend," they embraced him. "We pledge you by our epaulets and upon the sanctity of our honor that the general's terms will be carried out."

Padre de Lire, who had visited Colonel Fisher when he was ill with smallpox at Camargo, thrust in his plea "By the holy faith of the church this pledge will be kept." Then, lifting his eyes in a pious manner, he added, "My dear son, do not throw yourself away."

General Green raised his repeating rifle. "You men deserve death. You are violating military ethics."

"Hold on, there," cried Captain William Ryan, grasping the general's gun. "Wait, I pray you, until we learn what their intentions are."

Green slipped away from the group of schemers and spoke to Captain Cameron, "Form your company and make ready for further orders."

The Scot gathered his men, rifles in hand.

"Colonel Fisher," Green barked, "stand aside, I beg you, so that Cameron's company may fire into these intruders."

"No, general," he replied.

"Permit me then, colonel, to take these men prisoners. I will march them without harm at the head of our column to our camp on the other side of the Rio Grande. There, no matter what happens, we will be safe."[5]

Captain Reese, whose company was also in formation some forty yards away, came forward. "Yes, colonel, they will serve as informers against us. Let us take them prisoners."

Colonel Fisher shook his head.

Pleased by the concessions and the confusion among the Texans, one Mexican officer said, "We will

give you one hour in which to decide the matter."
They turned and walked off to safety.

The Texans were in an uproar. They complained that Colonel Fisher was ready to call off the fight because he was wounded. General Green should be placed in command. Green was right to have fired on the deceivers. If they surrendered, Santa Anna would have them all shot. The promises made by the Mexicans were worthless; they would end up murdering their prisoners.

General Green rushed about to talk with the officers. Some of them seemed inclined to accept surrender. He wanted to reason with them. He went to Captain Cameron. "Captain, is it possible that you favor a surrender?"

The big Scottish stone mason, who had come to Texas in 1836, choked at the mention of the word. Taking the general by the hand, he led him into the house where seven men from his company lay wounded on the floor Some moaned in their pain. Others cried out, "Hold on for the honor of our country." One fellow motioned to Green, holding up his pair of silver mounted pistols. "Take them, this is all I can do for you now." There were twenty-three wounded, one with both eyes shot out, lying among their dead comrades.

"What would you do, general?" asked Cameron, moved by the suffering.

"Men, if by staying here with you we could ease your pain or heal your wounds, I would say remain. But you will have the help of our doctors and will no doubt be treated as well if we go as if we surrendered. Either way we will be separated."[6]

Green crossed the plaza to talk with Captain Ryan, who replied, "Most of my company are for fighting it out."

At this point Captain Cameron hurried over and spoke harshly, passion accenting his Scottish dialect, "By God, general, me and the whole company will go it!"

Green then encountered Captains Reese and Pearson "How do you feel, boys?"

"Every man of us is for fighting."

"We're all for seeing it through."

"If we decided not to stand here, then we should fight our way out of Mier and down to the river," Green proposed. "Our probable loss would not exceed twenty. The high bank of the river would ward off cavalry charges and their infantry can't hurt us too much in that rough terrain. I will lead the fight through and pledge my life on the results!"

Colonel Fisher at the council of the officers asked General Green to go with him to General Ampudia's headquarters, but he replied, "You know how I feel, that I am firmly opposed to accepting their cursed white flag!"

So Fisher went alone and stayed fifty minutes. During his absence Green determined that not more than twenty favored surrender.

The companies were formed to hear Colonel Fisher's report. He repeated General Ampudia's offer and added "I have known General Pedro de Ampudia for years, I know him to be an honorable man and will vouch that he will carry out his promises. If you are willing to accept his terms, you will march into the public square and give up your arms or prepare for battle in five minutes; that, in any view of the case, your situation is gloomy one, for you cannot fight your way out of this place to the Rio Grande short of a loss of two-thirds, or perhaps the whole; but if you are determined to fight, I will be with you and sell my life as dear as possible."

It was fate that Fisher had been wounded at the critical moment. He was in no condition to face the enemy's subterfuge. Had he forgotten in his pain what Santa Anna did to Travis, Crockett, Bowie and their men at the Alamo, to Fannin at Goliad, to Dawson at Salado Creek and to the Santa Fe Expedition?

At the words of their commander nearly half of the men stepped away from their ranks and moved into the plaza. The others who stood firm broke into tears and oaths.

As the men passed the companies of Reese and Pearson, who refused to budge, bitter words were flung at them: "Go. I hope you may never enjoy the sight of your country and liberty again!"

"Go, you cowards! And rot in chains and slavery!"

Tom Green strode after them, waving his repeater. "I intend to shoot as many of the deserters as possible."

A gray-haired man grabbed his arm. "Control yourself, general. As an old friend I plead with you."

Green murmured, "We will all be sacrificed, but I will stand with you." He beat his sword upon the stone of the plaza. "Now we will see who can stand shooting best."

He turned to the Mexican surgeon and

snapped, "Please show me to General Ampudia."

Unloosing his sword belt, he advanced to the enemy commander, delivering it to him, "I am General Green. I have opposed the surrender in vain. I am prepared for prison or to be shot and am perfectly indifferent in the choice."[7]

General Ampudia bowed gravely, "I appreciate the feelings of the brave but yours is the fate of war. My house and friendship are yours. I hope you will consider yourself my guest. Call upon me freely for any service that is in my power to give."

Green turned back to look at the melancholy sight of the rifles piled upon the cobblestones and their former valiant bearers being herded together.

As Fisher's men walked forward to give up their arms, John and Asa Hill walked across to join Captain Cameron's company. More than forty men stood loyally by the Scot. "Keep on fighting, captain," they urged "We'll follow you to hell!"

But the contagion of defeat was in the air as Texans staggered out one by one. There was no way to stem the tide. Cameron gathered his men closer. "What shall we do?"

"Let's make a dash for it."

"We are forty against two thousand five hundred," groaned Cameron.

John gripped his gun as he watched the dance of the half-crazed Mexicans who were elated over their ruse and whose antics grew louder and more violent.

"My brother was massacred at Goliad. If we give in, they'll kill us sure," protested Big Foot Wallace.

Cameron shook his head. "There's no use,

boys. They've all gone but us and we'll have to knuckle under."

The Scot in his tartan led his men. Sadly and rebelliously they laid down their rifles, revolvers, knives, powder horns, catskin and tiger-tailed pouches, treasures that had been passed from fathers to sons or had been captured in other conflicts.

The thunderous cry of the Mexicans echoed through the plaza, *"Rindan sus armas! Rindanse!"* (Lay down your arms. Surrender!)

Big Foot Wallace was among the last, a scowling giant. He slumped forward in his beaten moccasins, bareheaded. He had broken up his fighting tools. "I have failed," he murmured, "to avenge the death of my kin!"

Asa plodded forward behind Big Foot, glancing back at John, who waited alone before an open doorway. He believed John would follow, but instead he remained there. He hoped he would not try anything desperate. One wounded son was enough.

The Mexicans had been watching every move of the Texans and now they turned their attention to the last of them, the youth who resisted their order. John clutched the rifle close to his body as he moved slowly. Suddenly alert, eyes flashing, he whirled his gun into the air, caught it by the barrel and struck the weapon on the stones of the pavement. The stock splintered into fragments while he stood defiant, with the barrel in his hands.

"I have kept my promise," he murmured.[8]

The gun barrel tumbled down with a clatter. He turned to lean against the plaza wall, face hidden against the ragged arm of his buckskin jacket.

John Christopher Columbus Hill breaking his rifle.
(Courtesy Texas State Library.)

Wheeling resolutely, he swung across the plaza to take his place beside Asa, so concerned with his disappointment that he did not sense what the enemy was shouting.

7

The Young Hero
Confronts General Ampudia

*T*HE MEXICANS ON THE ROOF TOPS, in doorways and
spilling into the plaza were intent on the conduct of the lad who was the last to surrender. They
did not know about his pledge, but the gesture of
courage appealed to their sporting sense. They broke
into a shout of applause, *"Pobrecito. Pobrecito. El tien
mucho valor."*

John glanced around at the hilarious enemy.
He was crestfallen over the Texans' humiliation and
bitter over the loss of the rifle.

"Come with me, little hero," a voice called in
Spanish. He swung about to face an officer who was
accompanied by a guard. "General Pedro de Ampudia asks that you appear before him at once."

Like his fellow Texans, John's brain reeled from
the trauma of the fierce battle and Ampudia's sudden
subterfuge, stampeding the invaders to surrender. He
turned to the swarthy-faced officer who waited beside
him with the shattering announcement that he must
face the supreme commander of the enemy. He would

have to account for the shooting of seventeen artillery men and the defiant gesture with his rifle.[1]

John gave no answer but fell in behind the lieutenant trailed by the armed soldier.

They entered the wrought iron gateway of Garcia Mansion on the opposite side of the square next to the church, passed through sentinels and up stone steps into a hallway. Here his guards muttered something to a petty officer who led them into a long drawing room before General Ampudia, seated in an armchair, regal in his uniform, rich with gold braid, epaulets, belt and sword. A medal clung about his neck. There was an array of decorations on his chest. He appeared dark, shaggy haired and bearded, sur- rounded by a confusing array of officers.

So this was the heroic captive? A mere child in rags. Ampudia noted the shapeless moccasins, tat- tered trousers and jacket and face stained with grime. Yet there was a bearing about the boy, evident in the grace of his features and alert posture. In one hand he clutched the remnants of a beaten felt hat, while the other was tightly closed.

"*Mi hijito*," the general reassured. "Do not be afraid. I shall not harm you."

Tense with anticipation of the worst, weak for lack of food and sleep, John did not sense the full meaning of Ampudia's intention, although he caught some of the Spanish. He managed to look steadily into Ampudia's face as one of the officers interpreted.

"*Queridito* (dear little fellow), come closer.'" The general held out his right hand. "What is your name?"

"John Christopher Columbus Hill."[2]

"Ah, Juan Christobal Colon Gil," the general repeated slowly, his eyes brightening. "A good Spanish name, but you are too young to be a soldier. Are the Texans so short of men that they must send their little ones into battle?"

"I am no little one," flashed John. "I am thirteen, going on to fourteen!"

"My apologies, señor," Ampudia returned. "I did not realize. It is a manly age indeed. What, may I ask, did you expect to discover in Mexico?"

"I came to fight Mexicans."

"But why? We are not such evil men."

"Because we Texans must be free."

"There seems little doubt in your mind about that. But what about all the good things the Spanish have done in your world to the north?"

"But Texans are part of a new world that will not be ruled by Mexico or any other power."

"How many Texans are there?"

"About twenty thousand."

"And you expect to hold your own against eight million Mexicans?"

"You can judge by our marksmanship."

"As a military man I wish I had a regiment of such riflemen." A look of sadness came over the general "My own son, Don Miguel Arsenal, a graduate of Chapultepec Military College, Adjutant General of our forces, the pride of my life, lies close to death. He was shot through the kidneys and there is no hope for him. I know how deadly your Texan fire is and how tragic are the losses of war."

"I am sorry, sir."

"You have no father?"

"Yes, sir, he is here in the plaza prison and also my brother, Jeffrey."

"Why is it that you had to go with your father and brother? Would it not have been better for you to have stayed at home with your mother?"

"I came along to help them. My other brothers are at home taking care of the family. It was my turn to go this time. James Monroe fought at San Jacinto, where we defeated Santa Anna. I was not old enough to go then, but this time I was."

General Ampudia studied him. "Captain Castro reported that you were one of the boys who shot down his entire battery."

"General Green ordered the five of us to take care of the cannon. 'Aim carefully and pick them off one by one,' he said."

"You succeeded, much to my regret. Only Captain Castro remains uninjured out of sixty gunners. Practically every man was shot through the brain. It is terrifying to think that you boys did this."

"I think I took care of about seventeen."

"And what are the names of the other boys?" John hesitated.

"Go ahead. I will not harm them."

"Orlando Phelps, Billie Reese, Harvey Sellers and Gilbert Brush."

"Slower please, repeat those names again." The general nodded to one of the officers and delivered a series of orders in Spanish. He then turned to John and placed his hand on his head. "You are a brave boy and so are your companions. I want you to follow this orderly. He will see that you have food and rest."

General Pedro De Ampudia.
(Courtesy University of Texas at Austin.)

"But what about my father and brother?" John clutched at his deerskin belt.

"They will be taken care of. All the Texans will be sheltered and fed."

"But Jeffrey is wounded."

"I will ask my surgeon to watch over him."

"And my father?"

"*Hombrecito*, I will see that they are protected. And in the morning you can see them both. Trust me, Don Juan. I intend to care for you as if you were my own son." (The general in translating his name into its Spanish equivalent addressed him as Don Juan, the term Don being used before one of equal rank.) "*Hasta Luego.*"

Dazed by his encounter, he followed the orderly across the plaza to a square stucco house. On returning to the house where he had been placed, John discovered that general Ampudia's guard had released the other fire eaters from imprisonment with the men and brought them to the building where he was lodged. Pleased over their transfer, the boys wanted to know how he had been treated by the enemy. He described his visit in Garcia Mansion and Ampudia's offer.

They were confused by the sudden change. Yesterday they were locked in deadly battle; today it was all over. They thought they were winning the fight, yet they were now prisoners of the enemy. It was the day after Christmas. The dead still lay about the square The boys ate the food the *mozos* brought them and fell asleep in their strange quarters.

* * * * * * *

After they had been disarmed the Texans were crowded into three buildings with a heavy guard set about them. The wounded were taken to the church which had been converted into a hospital. The field officers and the fire eaters were on parole and were not locked up. The men's baggage was pillaged, leaving them destitute of everything except the clothes on their backs. They were bare-armed and bare-headed, begrimed with smoke and powder, without bedding and ill equipped for the cold. About midnight small rations of boiled beef was brought them.[3]

"After the surrender a court martial was convened by General Ampudia to determine what was to be done with the captives. In defiance of the written articles of capitulation and the promises of Ampudia, this military inquisition sentenced every prisoner to be instantly shot. But General Ampudia dissented. About one-third of the Texans were ordered to prepare for marching. They were conducted across the square and at the entrance of a back yard surrounded by a high wall, every man was dispossessed of his knife, which he had been allowed to retain, and formed in single file with their backs against the wall, while a file of soldiers was formed facing them with loaded muskets and fixed bayonets. After standing in their tense situation for some minutes, they were escorted to their quarters," so wrote Thomas W. Bell, a member of the expedition.[4]

By this narrow margin the company escaped what had been meted out to Fannin and Dawson. The morning following the battle an orderly brought breakfast to the fire eaters. He told John that he was to eat with the general at the mansion. Ampudia then gave him some Mexican clothes to put on, with money in the pockets, and was pleased with his appearance. He told John that he was in Mexico now and should try to learn the ways of the country. This puzzled the boy, who wondered what he intended to do with him. Was he going to be held as hostage?

He asked if he could see his father and brother. Ampudia consented and sent servants along to carry the food. John set out with the orderly, accompanied by two *mozos* with trays of bread and coffee, across the plaza to the church where the wounded prisoners were quartered.

Soldiers were at work, moving the bodies of the dead. Ox carts were being loaded with corpses. Other victims were being lowered by ropes from the roof tops.[5]

John found Jeffrey in the church laid out with the wounded on the stone floor. The Mexicans had robbed him of most of his clothing. He asked John to please buy him a pair of trousers and to bring him a jug of water to help check his fever.

John was led by his escort to Asa, who was locked up in one of the buildings. After dispensing food to him and the hungry men there he told the story of his visits with Ampudia. He was a sensation to the Texans in his Mexican costume. They gleaned mild encouragement from his report of the enemy commander's treatment of their chief officers and the fire eaters.

Dr. Sinnickson congratulated John on landing on his feet, on being awarded his handsome new outfit, and on securing food for the troops. The doctor worked among the wounded and the disheartened prisoners instead of nursing his regret. He was blamed for carrying the white flag and betraying his people. He refused to give up under criticism and took the lead in striving to build up the morale of those who had been deceived.[5]

The church bells tolled for the departed souls. The carts still gathered up dead bodies and creaked mournfully about the plaza. It was estimated that the Texans had entered Mier with 265 men, of whom 13 had been killed in action and 18 wounded. The Mexican force of approximately 3,200 lost 600 dead and an undetermined number of wounded.[6]

8

Deceit and Humiliation

FOLLOWING THE SIGNING of the surrender papers, General Ampudia announced that he planned to dispatch cavalry to make prisoners of the Texans who had been left on the north side of the Rio Grande encamped with their horses and supplies. Colonel Fisher volunteered to send one of his men along to show the Mexicans the way. This was a ruse to deliver a warning to the men so they would not be captured.

General Green asked if he might have Sailing Master Lyon make the journey in order to secure his journal, papers and maps that he wished to carry with him. Ampudia consented. When the party reached the river, Lyon bellowed in a voice that was accustomed to give orders in a storm at sea, "Boys, we are all prisoners. There are several hundred cavalry close by in pursuit of you. Take all the good horses and put!"[1]

By the time the Mexicans crossed over they found nothing but a few broken nags, old saddle bags and cast off duffel. The booty was brought back to the plaza of Mier and placed on display for the conquerors to examine. The Mexicans were proud of it and were not told that forty-two men, the good horses and everything of value were galloping north toward home.

With Colonel Fisher wounded and his captains locked up, Tom Green confided with the fire eaters as his only counsel. He told them that he had received a copy of the order of the capitulation in writing. It was now apparent what he had suspected all the time, that General Canales had tricked them and written in words that permitted the enemy to evade their solemn pledge.

Green read to them in an angry voice, "Agreeable to the conference I had with Colonel W. S. Fisher, I have decided to grant:

"First. That all who will give up their arms will be treated with the consideration which is in accordance with the magnanimous Mexican nation.

"Second. That conforming to the petition which said General Fisher has made me, all persons belonging to the Santa Fe Expedition (another group of Texans who had been captured by the Mexicans before the battle of Mier) will receive the same treatment and guarantees as the rest.

"Third. All who desire to avail themselves of these terms will enter the square and there deliver up their arms. Pedro D'Ampudia.

"When the interpreter read the first article the words, 'with the consideration which is in accordance with the magnanimous Mexican nation' was given in different sense. He said, 'With all the honor and consideration of prisoners of war.' Never trusting a Mexican promise, I suggested to Fisher that it would be better for us to make use of our own interpreter. But he stated that he could read and understand the Spanish and he could see no objection to the written words. You can see now, can't you, that we have no pledge to be treated as prisoners of war, but only with 'the consideration which is in accordance with the magnanimous Mexican nation,' which is no promise at all They can shoot us or march us to Mexico City."[2]

General Green paced the room. "This is a case of irony of fate. Instead of calling a council of our officers, I must come here as a prisoner to talk it over with my youthful fire eaters. At least I can say this much for you lads, you have never been afraid to fight and that is the way to win a battle. With three hundred like you I could have trimmed these thirty-two hundred Mexicans! That swine of a Canales has tricked us, and once he is in cahoots with Santa Anna they will try every device of the devil on us."

"Can't we force General Ampudia to keep his word and set us free?" the boys asked.

"He is the best of the lot," replied the blunt general, "and he seems to be decent to those of us who are lucky enough to be quartered here. But he is treating our men like dogs. I have been visiting them crowded together in miserable places. They would still be willing to fight, if we could get the arms. Last night I was at the church with our wounded and l could sense their fighting spirit. 'How are you for rations?' I asked. They replied, 'Oh! we have plenty of brains!' One hundred and thirty-six of the enemy's wounded were laid out in the church near them, most of them shot in the head, their brains oozing out, chunks the size of marbles up to as big as my fist. We outfought them, but they outsmarted us."[3]

After proper masses had been said for the

dead, Padre Garcia, the local priest in charge of the
church, announced that they would hold a *feria* of
ten days' duration in celebration of their victory. The
plaza, only a few hours before flowing with blood,
was now alive with soldiers and peasants who jos-
tled one another, intent on craning at the booths that
had suddenly sprung up. The prisoners chafed at
their long confinement as they waited for some
announcement of their fate, embittered by the emo-
tional outpouring of the native people who reveled
over their betrayal.

Early on New Year's Day the Texans were
lined up for departure from Mier. The fair was at its
peak and the countryside flocked in to watch the foreign bandits. Peasants squatted on the ground
wrapped in their blankets under broad sombreros,
while pretty maidens peered from their *rebozos*. The
cavalry moved on fine horses, the sun playing on silver bridles, short swords and gleaming spurs. The
cavalrymen enjoyed parading in uniforms resplen-
dent with gold and silver braid and lace, riding in
their leather saddles. Officers shouted orders. The
Zapadores military band blazed away. Peddlers wove
about among the throng, shouting their wares: chile
con carne, candied fruits, sweetmeats, along with the
ever-present *tortillas*. Venders hawked their *frijoles*.
The *pulque* salesman carried an inflated pig skin, dol-
ing out the national drink to the celebrants of the
feria. Two wheel carts with great pancake wheels,
loaded with corn and pumpkins and pulled by oxen,
creaked along the crowded way, adding to the con-
gestion. The plaza was agog with excitement as the
populace turned out to gape at the *gringos*.

The prisoners were grateful to be in the sun after their days of imprisonment, but apprehensive as to the next move of their wily captors.

The cavalcade of men and beasts assembled amid the confusion. The Mexican officers were mounted and trailed by *burros* that were loaded with equipment. All that could be seen of the mouse gray creatures was slender legs as they waited under their hills of luggage. The Texans were formed in platoons and placed in the center of an oblong formation with lines of infantry on both sides, and beyond them columns of cavalry. In front was one six-pound cannon with artillerymen, cavalry and the general and his staff. At the rear were other pieces of ordinance manned by their troops.[4]

The caravan moved at last with wild shouting and waving from the citizens of Mier. General Ampudia signaled for John to ride beside him on the mustang he had given him. The other boys were assigned to the rear with Captain Castro. As they passed among the watching crowd a sudden silence fell over the marchers. There was the pulsation of feet on the dusty roadway, the clump of horses' hoofs, the jangle of bits and spur. The men who trudged between the rows of Mexican bayonets were depressed with thoughts of the journey that lay before them. Shut up in cramped quarters for six days without exercise or proper food, they plodded in their shabby riding boots and moccasins.

They hoped that they were moving north toward San Antonio but soon realized that they were going southeast. It was apparent that Ampudia was taking them to his home city of Matamoros. The Texans began to speculate about making a break there. Matamoros was near the mouth of the Rio Grande and close to the sea. What had happened to Ampudia's bargain that he would keep them on the border until they could be exchanged and sent home?

Whiskered footmen trudged along with drums, fife and horns that thundered forth the renown of the Mexican arms. The brown country stretched before them as far as the eye could reach. The road wound in and out among stunted clumps of thorny vines and shrubs that formed the dreaded chaparral. Loose sand had drifted across the trail and men and animals sank into it with each step. Cacti grew giant-like, ready to prick and sting all who brushed against them.

As John's horse bore him along he was suddenly jolted by a sharp, pricking blow from a lance flung at his left shoulder. He glanced about and saw a young Mexican private glowering at him and muttering, "Die Yankee devil!"

John swung out of the moving column as two officers pounced on the assailant. The Mexican surgeon examined John and bound up the slight wound, which fortunately did not become infected.[5]

Ampudia was insistent that no time be permitted for stops during the morning because they must reach Camargo by nightfall. The guards pushed the prisoners and allowed no pause even for water.

By noon they made a *hacienda*, a little colony of adobe houses built about an open square. They marched in through the great double gates in the walls that had been built to keep out the wild beasts and the *ladrones*. A stream flowed through the courtyard, forming an oasis with cottonwood and ratama trees that hovered about the buildings.

During the brief halt John saw Asa, one of the few Texans who was fortunate enough to be able to ride. John had persuaded Ampudia to give his father a horse.

After a twenty-five mile march the cavalcade crept into Camargo in the winter twilight with a bleak norther blowing. The prisoners were doled out a meager supply of half-boiled beef. They dropped down on the cold ground with the sky for a covering as the winter wind swirled dust about them. Their blankets had been stolen by the cavalry. John and the boys were led, with the commanding officers, to the home of Don Trinidad. Their window in the big house looked out onto a patio shaded by orange and lemon trees.

The next day Captain Castro walked with Tom Green and the boys through the streets of Camargo which were filled with crowds assembled to celebrate the great victory over the Texans.

Castro said to General Green, "I don't want to subject you to humiliation. Would it be better for us to avoid the plaza?"

"Let's go ahead," exclaimed the general stoutly. "We came to see everything."

The parade was underway.

A company of children marched by, holding a banner over their heads:

ETERNAL HONOR A LA IMMORTA AMPUDIA
Another group followed with a huge paper scroll:

GLORIA Y
GRATITUD A AL
BRAVO CANALES

The crowds shouted "Viva" while the band blared away with rousing rhythm. Firecrackers banged and the bell in the church added its clamor.[6]

In the morning the other prisoners were paraded through the streets and compelled to make circuits of the public square for the entertainment of the citizens and the glorification of the captors. They were presented as the first specimens of *espantoso* Texans who had ever appeared in the valley of the Rio Grande. They were regarded with as cautious and severe scrutiny as the natives would have bestowed on the same number of winged griffins. They were herded into line while the crowd gaped and chattered.

Ampudia rode at the forefront as they moved on, with John near by. The general bowed and smiled to the *vivas* of the people, but the boy passed in silence through the bedlam, sensing what his friends were enduring, and worrying about his father and brother. General Green boiled with resentment. Colonel Fisher was conscious of the criticism the men were heaping upon him for his acceptance of the Mexican terms.

General Ampudia looked after John and inquired about his welfare. As he moved along John heard the people speak of him as "General Ampudia's son."

The prisoners plodded slowly and heavily, their feet swollen from the long march from Mier. At the close of a ten-mile stretch it was decided to stop and make quarters at a ranch. There were no buildings large enough to take care of the prisoners, so they were turned into a corral, a large yard enclosed by upright and close-set pickets; the lower ends set firmly in the ground, the tops of the uprights bound together by rawhide strips to the horizontal timbers.

The Texans snorted at the cow pen, the hog wallow hotel that Ampudia offered them and their entertainment with all the honor of prisoners of war. They were being "treated with consideration which is in accordance with the magnanimous Mexican nation." Although disgusted by the humiliation, some kept their sense of humor. They dropped down on hands and knees, pawed the ground, lowed like cows and bellowed like bulls while others bleated like hungry calves.

The Mexican guard shrank back frightened at the antics of their captives. Were they drunk? Or had they gone insane? At last they sensed that the Texans were making fun of a bad situation and burst into laughter.

Continuing their route down the river, they reached New Reinosa, some fifty miles from Camargo, and halted there on the afternoon of January 4. The streets were embellished with banners and flags and another *feu de joie* waited them. They walked under triumphal arches built of reeds and ornamented by bright handkerchiefs, shawls and petticoats. Following a melodramatic parade three times around the square, they were quartered for the night in a huge unfinished brick building on the edge of the town.[7]

The excitement of the Indian demonstrators took their minds off their problems for a few minutes. The prisoners were marched from the plaza into the church and compelled to stand for two hours through mass. There were no pews or benches. They grew restless and rebellious standing on the cold stone floor listening to a service in an alien tongue.

This dictatorial move brought vigorous protest such as, "No one can make me go into a Roman Catholic church." But the omnipresent guard with their bayonets had their way. After two days in New Reinosa they departed on the morning of January 6. As they approached Matamoros the country became more inviting. The rolling prairies were dressed in rich and nutritious muskeet grasses, thickly studded with timber and filled with numerous herds of fine looking cattle, the property of more wealthy and substantial farmers than those that they had passed.[8]

As the journey lengthened on toward Matamoros, stage coaches of friends and relatives drove out to greet the returning Mexican army. Many of the soldiers were from this area. Wives and sweethearts came to see their men. Some learned that their loved ones had been killed at Mier and crept mournfully home to pray for their souls before a crucifix.

The troops were met by a multitude of men, women and children, all eager for a glimpse of the spectacle. Little donkeys, scarcely taller than Newfoundland dogs, carried long-legged riders. *Arrieros* appeared with strings of mules, loaded with inquisitive children. Women venders with *tortillas* and fruit for sale, curates, blacklegs and *leperos* mingled with carts and carriages in the motley concourse.

The city of Matamoros was gay with triumphal signs and garlands. Troops from the military quarters in fresh uniforms lined the roads. They made their way through a cheering throng to the cathedral where another mass was sung to commemorate the victory. Captain Castro escorted the boys, the commanding officers and their aides to Ampudia's headquarters while the other captives were paraded through the streets to impress the people with the conquest that had been made over the foreign foe. General Ampudia was roundly condemned by his prisoners for this vanity, lack of good taste and disregard for military ethics.

During the week they passed in Matamoros the military supplied them with better food and citizens contributed supplies of clothing that were sorely needed. These donations came from foreign merchants and from the local gentry. Prisoners were permitted to write letters home.[9]

General Ampudia thought of his son and the others he had left behind at Mier. He was also distressed by the orders from Santa Anna that he found awaiting him at his headquarters:

"All Texan prisoners captured at Mier are to be forwarded immediately via Monterey to the City of Mexico. The Texan leaders are to be sent in advance as hostages for the behavior of the men."[10]

Ampudia had promised Fisher that he would prevent the Texans from being shipped to the interior. It was soon evident that he would take no stand to defend this pledge. The news reached the prisoners who had been separated into three groups and confined behind iron bars in utter darkness with nothing but the floor for beds. Outside they heard the tramping sentinel calling, *"Centinela alerta,"* the hunting phrase they had already learned to dread.

Ampudia announced that Santa Anna had given the command as supreme head of the government that all prisoners should be marched to Mexico City and that the commanding officers should be sent ahead and held hostages to insure the good conduct of their men.

Colonel Fisher and General Green confronted General Ampudia. "We are distressed to know that your terms have been repudiated, general," Fisher said. "This is contrary to all military ethics."

"I regret this deeply, gentlemen," Ampudia stated. "I, too, have passed a sleepless night."

"Knowing you as we did," Colonel Fisher went on, "I committed my men to you and relied upon your integrity."

"On my honor I had no idea that General Santa Anna would override me in this manner. I was shocked to receive this order."

"General Santa Anna dislikes me with a vengeance," said General Green. "I hope it is not because of me personally that he has taken this vengeful attitude. Colonel Fisher and I will gladly serve as hostages and go in advance to Mexico City if it will afford any protection to our men."

"But the report that they are to march in irons to Mexico City," broke in Fisher hotly, "that is outrage. Surely you will not permit such barbarous treatment of your prisoners of war!"

"General Canales, the officer who is to conduct the prisoners to Monterey insisted upon having them ironed," explained General Ampudia. "He stated that he would not undertake to guard two hundred and twenty Texans with less than one thousand Mexican troops. But I will overrule that order as a violation of the articles of capitulation."

"Thank you, general," answered Fisher. "I only wish that you could counteract the march to Mexico City and permit our men to remain here on the border as originally promised and be exchanged as soon as possible."

"Your regret is no deeper than my own," General Ampudia returned. "I will allow you two days to prepare yourselves for the journey, gentlemen."

On January 12 Colonel Fisher sent a message to the Texans:

"Let us bear up under our privations with the fortitude of men. Let us nerve our souls in that impregnable armour which lightens the weary limb, and which the steel of our enemy cannot penetrate. That immortal spirit will make us superior to our condition and triumph over our misfortunes. A long and weary journey lies before us. The gloom of the prison and the fatigues of this thousand miles of space we embrace are pleasures in a comparison to this cruel separation from you, who have so nobly battled for your country and shared every danger."

General Ampudia called Fisher and Green to warn them, "The report comes to me that your men are planning to charge their guard and try to escape. You must go by the prison and inform them that if they take this action your lives will be forfeited."

In spite of the order Fisher spoke to Captain Cameron, "Do what you think best and try to escape if you can. Use your own judgment in the matter."

Green told them right and left, "Let no opportunity slip by in overpowering your guards and getting home. Do so regardless of any consequences to me."

The mounted company, including Colonel

Fisher General Green, their two aides, Adjutant Murray and Sailing Master Lyon and jolly Dan Henrie, as
interpreter, set out on January 12. They were guarded
by Lieutenant Colonel Savriego and forty cavalrymen. On the tenth day they reached Monterey, a distance of 275 miles.[11]

Two days after their departure John watched
his father and his unhappy comrades as they set out
on foot to the journey to the Mexican capital.

The fire eaters were compelled to go along.
Ampudia had promised to send them home from
Matamoros but he backed down on this pledge when
Santa Anna ordered the prisoners south. On being
reminded of his agreement, he said, "If I send you
home now you will be back upon the Rio Grande in
three weeks, fighting again."

General Canales, who insisted that the Texans
should wear irons, was angry because Ampudia
rescinded his order. The stern Canales maintained
irksome police control over the prisoners and at all
times kept a safe and contemptuous distance from
them, never coming within a hundred yards.

John had been placed in school by General
Ampudia with Asa's consent, where he was registered
as John Christobal Colon Gil de Ampudia. The general
and his family were kind to him and he felt honor
bound to continue as an adopted son as long as he
could aid Asa and Jeffrey and the Texans. He managed
to secure a horse for his father to make the journey to
Mexico City easier. He had collected some money to
help him an other prisoners buy food enroute.

John waved farewell to his father as the
depressing cavalcade departed, and ran to General

Ampudia's mansion to hide his tears. He would have wept more bitterly if he had known that Asa's horse had been taken from him after the retinue had moved a short distance from the city. General Canales issued the order that *all* Texans were to proceed on foot.

Left alone in Matamoros, John explored the city, wandering among the dwellings with their iron-barred gates, set in brick walls, covered with stucco and painted rose, blue and yellow. He watched the people in the patios drinking their coffee and pulque. He followed carts that creaked through the streets, loaded with pumpkins, gourds, corn, baskets and pottery stopping to watch a cock fight or a column of soldiers drilling under wide sombreros.

In an effort to fight off loneliness and anxiety about his father and Jeffrey, John plunged into his studies. He wrote to his mother, reporting on the strange alien life that surrounded his adopted home. As he struggled to adapt to his difficult situation, the daily routine was suddenly interrupted by the shocking news Señor Ampudia read to him. It came in a letter from President Santa Anna:

"I request that the young Texan, Juan Christobal Colon Gil, be sent on to me under safe guard by way of Tampico and Rio del Monte to Mexico City."

The general could not tell him what *El Presidente* had in mind. Was he to be punished in the capital because he had shot so many of the artillerymen at Mier? Why would Santa Anna single him out among the prisoners?

Ampudia had formed a deep attachment to John, who had come into his life in such a dramatic fashion. He loved the handsome lad, who, like a divine gift, had helped soothe the anguish over the loss of his own son at the battle of Mier.

The general had presented John with a beautiful horse and saddle, decorated after the Mexican fashion, and now with his own hands assisted him onto his mount.[12]

The officers about the headquarters had assembled to bid goodbye to the protege of the general. The young traveler turned in his saddle, moving his hand, and with a grateful heart returned to the general and other officers a pathetic parting salutation, "Adios."

Pedro de Ampudia had lost control over his adopted son and over Asa and Jeffrey when Santa Anna commanded him to send them to Mexico City. The horse he had given Asa to ride was seized by Canales who forced Asa to walk the long, agonizing journey to the capital. He was no longer able to keep his promise to return Asa and Jeffrey safely home.

John's Arrival in Mexico City

*A*S THE JOURNEY BROUGHT THEM to the country that surrounded the capital, John looked down on the site chosen by the Aztecs, a valley some fifty miles long and forty miles wide, the floor of an ancient volcano, 7,500 feet above the sea. Set among lakes and canals, it had won the title of the Venice of the West. After the Spanish conquerors concluded their bombardment of the ancient city and the massacre of its inhabitants, they rebuilt on their European pattern.

The captain delivered John and his little equipage at the National Palace. Word was relayed to the gate that the president was ill and that the boy captive was to stay temporarily in the palace of the archbishop next to the cathedral nearby on the great plaza. John was left in the care of a young friar who led him into the residence of the religious leader of the nation. Their steps echoed through the corridors. The marble walls were hung with paintings and portraits and embellished with statuary. A cool and shadowy mystery pervaded the stately structure.

Archbishop Manual Posada stepped forward from his desk in silk robes and took John's hand in

Archbishop Manuel Posada.
(Courtesy University of Texas at Austin.)

his soft palm. "My young friend, *El Presidente* told me that you would be coming. He is sick just now. You are to stay here with me until he is able to see you. Let us know what you need. You must be weary after your long journey."[1]

Relieved by this welcome, John explained that he was accustomed to riding a horse but that he was concerned about his father and brother and the other Texans who were mistreated.

The cleric placed his hand on the boy's head, saying, "My son, these things are in the hands of God We must pray to the Holy Mother to intercede and bring your dear ones to you safely."

The friar took John to a bedroom where he was installed for his stay with the Roman Catholic pontiff. The next day the youthful guest was shown the cathedral that had been started in 1425, built on the site of the temple of Montezuma. He stood before the figure of the Virgin of Remedios in her dress of diamonds and precious stones and climbed the steep stairs to the tower to see the famous bell named Santa Maria de Guadalupe. Below him lay the avenues of the city, the canals and lake and beyond the snow-clad mountains, the grand peak Popocatepetl, called Old Popo because he was said to be the husband of Ixteccihautl, the white woman. Chapultepec was pointed out—the spot where Montezuma built his summer palace. Within the park of cypress trees hung with silver moss stood the Military Academy.

John was ushered into the reception hall of the cathedral complex to wait for a talk with Archbishop Posada. Other visitors were there also, so he was seated near the front window where he could look out on the plaza. He heard the buzz of voices from below and peered through the iron balcony.

Someone on the street rang a bell and called, *"Dios viene! Dios viene!"* The spectators dropped to their knees on the pavement. A coach rolled up drawn by well groomed mules. A priest sat inside in dignified silence and behind him walked a dozen chanting friars with lighted candles. At the sound of the bell the visitors in the room knelt and murmured so rapidly that John could not catch their words. At the rumble of protest behind him he turned to see Archbishop Posada, who also knelt with bowed head. An angry attendant stared at John, who waited in confusion not realizing what was expected of him.[2]

From the street he heard the tinkle of tiny bells and the solemn chant of the priests. The procession passed on and still he waited, puzzled.

"Good day, my son," sounded the deep voice of the archbishop who spoke a hasty word to the attendant. When John turned to him they were alone.

The archbishop's eyes studied him. "My son, although you rejected the Holy Mother, do you not accept the Holy Son, our Lord Jesus Christ?"

"Yes, of course," John faltered.

"Then why do you not make your devotions when He passes by on his way to the faithful dying?"

"I do not understand. I am not familiar with this custom."

"It was the host that was passing in procession. The holy sacrament is being carried to comfort one near death. The dying confesses his sins to the priest, receives forgiveness and then partakes of the bread and the wine."

"I am sorry, I did not intend to be disrespect-ful."

"My son, you must be baptized by the true church. Then you will understand the beauty of the faith. I will appoint a time in the near future for you to be baptized."

"Baptized!" John echoed. "When I was a baby I was baptized in the Methodist Church and later I was confirmed. It is the church of my parents, the Hill family, and all my people. I can never leave it."

"But John, do you not realize that unless you belong to *the* Church, you may be cast into eternal punishment? Our Lord made it clear when he spoke of St. Peter, 'On this rock I will build my church and the gates of hell shall not prevail against it.' It was in Rome, where St. Peter was martyred, that the Holy Church was established and we have through the centuries, because of the apostolic succession, remained the only Church that can save the souls of men."

John was dismayed by the words of the learned churchman. When the archbishop had finished he asked, "Do you mean that those who do not believe in your church will not go to heaven when they die?"

"Yes, that is certain, my son."

"But I don't understand how God can be so unjust as to shut out such good people as my mother and the rest of my relatives. If they can't get to heaven then I want to go where they go."

Archbishop Posada was silent for a moment. "The Holy Mother loves a good son, and God is merciful," he added gently.

John groped with the strange concepts. "These mysteries are beyond us and in the care of God,"

Posada continued. "From now on you will remember that when the Sacred Host is carried past, you should uncover your head and bow. If you do not, the ignorant people may turn upon you because you fail to show respect for their beliefs."

As he explored the streets John found churches, convents and monasteries all around him with their priests, nuns and begging friars. It was Lent and people flowed in and out of the cathedral and lesser shrines, dipped into holy water, crossed themselves and knelt for prayer. There was a procession of *caballeros*, dressed in dashing elegance, *senoritas* in frilly lace with their more sedate mothers, graceful with *mantillas* and fans, country women in blue cotton and black *rebozos*.

John was dazzled by the beautiful trees, shrubs, flowers and plants, which he beheld in the archbishop's garden. There were fine, old olive trees which the friar assured him were brought from Europe; grand banana plants, and many lemon and orange trees, and clinging to every possible support were rare, large, double, red and pink roses, and white and yellow jasmine filled the air with fragrance; camellias, violets, japonicas, carnations, hibiscus and a bewildering array of gorgeous vines and flowers which he had never before seen, greeted his eyes at every turn.

In contrast with the peace of the garden were streets teaming with peasants. The water carriers with their heavy jars seemed to have the right-of-way; their peculiar manner of strapping their burthen around their forehead prevented them from looking up and avoiding obstacles in their path.

Little mouse-colored burros loaded with charcoal were guided on their tortuous path by half-naked Indians yelling *'Carbon! Carbon!'* (charcoal). In another direction long lines of little burros crept slowly on their way loaded with wood, vegetables, corn, jars, baskets, anything and everything that was used in the domestic life of the Mexican.

Many of the men had panniers of vegetables and others had tall coops full of poultry, cackling and crowing in the most animated fashion as if discussing their first impressions of the city.

Indians were plentiful, swinging along at a little dog trot with big baskets or crates loaded with fruit or vegetables, or a wardrobe or bureau, everything, in fact, that the burro (donkey) carries except timber or wood. The peddlers of *pulque* presented a very odd appearance indeed for they carried this popular beverage in the skin of a sheep or pig, even the legs in entirety.

In his big and lonely bedroom John wondered why the archbishop spoke about arranging to have him baptized? Was this part of a plot to prepare him for his punishment? Could that be the reason why Santa Anna had put him under the care of Posada? Nights were long in the empty silence of the palace with the whispering of prayers and the sounding of bells.

John received a letter from General Ampudia that came by a government courier. It was addressed:

A Juan C. C. Hill de Ampudia
Palacio Nacional Mexico

A letter was enclosed from John's mother.

The general continued to write him for many years, using the name he had given him at Matamoros and always calling him "*mi querido hijito*."

Finally a message came from the Presidential Palace. The friar announced, "His Excellency, El Señor General Presidente Antonio Lopez de Santa Anna wishes to see Señor Juan Christobal Colon Gil, the Texas boy."

An aide from the president's staff had been dispatched with the order to escort the captive from the archbishop's palace into the presence of the supreme figure of Mexico. John was to face the dictator who was feared by every Texan, the murderer of Travis, Bowie and Crockett at the Alamo, of Fannin and his men at Goliad, of Dawson and his company at Salado Creek. He had broken Ampudia's promises and was dragging the betrayed Texans across the country on foot over countless miles as if they were the lowest of criminals. He must be a tyrant or why would he take him away from Pedro de Ampudia?

The aide escorted him across the *Calle de Moneda* from the archbishop's palace to the National Palace that fronted on the *Zocalo*. It stood on the site of the palace of Montezuma—a three-story structure about 500 feet in length and 350 in width. Ambassador Waddy Thompson said that its imposing stone and narrow window made it look like a cotton factory or penitentiary. John studied the building, speculating on what the president inside looked like.

Today the guards saluted him as he passed through the gates. Up the steps they made their way and down a hallway coming at last into a vast and shadowy room hung with portraits of great men. He made out one that he recognized, a lifesize figure of George Washington. The aide was leading him forward to a platform where Santa Anna waited.

The blond, blue-eyed boy stared at his face, olive complexion, black hair brushed back from above well formed ears onto a broad forehead. His mouth and chin were firmly set.

The president stood, an impressive figure in red and gold. "Well, my friend, I have heard about you. Although still very young, you have made a reputation for yourself."[3]

John waited, hands tense at his sides.

"General Ampudia has told me about your actions at Mier. Not many boys could have conducted themselves as you have."

"I only did my duty as a Texan," John managed to reply.

"You are brushing aside your accomplishments with too much modesty." *El Presidente* bowed toward two dignified gentlemen who appeared through a doorway. "Don Juan, may I introduce General Jose Maria Tornel, Minister of War."

"Welcome to Mexico," General Tornel greeted him in English. "I spent some time in the United States as ambassador." In his high-collared uniform, with heavy black hair and long sideburns, he was very handsome This well groomed, literary man was called Lorenzo the Magnificent.

"And this," Santa Anna continued, "is Vice President Valentin Gomez Farias."

The vice president shook John's hand. This scholar and liberal had worked for reform in Mexico when Santa Anna had first been elected president as

General Antonio Lopez Santa Ana.
(Courtesy Texas State Library.)

a liberal, but he soon developed conservative views. Farias held more progressive ideas. He had made a trip to New Orleans where he conferred with Lorenzo Zavala and other Mexicans who opposed Santa Anna's policies and were working for the Republic of Texas. He had sympathized with the Texans.

"I have asked these gentlemen to come here for few minutes to talk with me about your future," Santa Anna went on. "I admire your courage and resourcefulness. I ordered General Ampudia to send you here because I would like to adopt you as my son."

El Presidente explained that he would be pleased to place him in the Military Academy at Chapultepec where he would be provided with an education and become an officer.

"I appreciate your kindness, Mr. President. I would be glad to attend one of your schools but as to being adopted as your son, I have my own father and mother. I would not serve in your army. If war should break out between Texas and Mexico I would go home and support my own people. I would never fight against my own country."

"If you do not wish to become a student at Chapultepec, where would you like to study?" Santa Anna asked.

"Sir, I cannot give you an answer until l know about my father and brother. I do not want to make any promises until l know they are safe. I made a pledge to my mother that I would take care of them. I did the best I could while I was with them. Before I agreed to live with General Ampudia, he promised to help them. He gave father a horse to ride from Mier to Matamoros. When you ordered our men to be marched to Mexico City he provided him with a horse, but General Canales took it from him. Today he may be lying along some roadside. And Jeff may still be suffering with his wound. I dream about them every night. I am alone in this country cut off from my family. I fear I will never see them again."[4]

"*Mi hijito*, try not to grieve so deeply. I will do all in my power to help them. In the meantime I want you to come to the palace and be as a son to me and my wife, Dona Inez. We shall do all that we can to comfort you."

"But, Mr. President, will you give them their freedom and send them home to Texas?" John stood his ground.

The brusque and venturesome military commander, who was accustomed to give orders, was pleased by the determined spirit of his captive, and answered, "Yes, when they come and your father consents for you to remain and accept an education, and you are willing to do so, then I will liberate them both and send them home safely to your mother. And what about your choice of schools?" Santa Anna asked.

"I think I would like to be in one of your schools. Once father arrives and gives consent to all this, I will be willing."

General Tornel, director of the Mineria, an old college founded by Spaniards for the sons of miners an mine owners, said, "Your Excellency, I think our young friend would like the Mineria. If you will permit me I shall be pleased to have him come into my family and attend the college with my two boys. In this way I shall have three sons and he shall have two nationalities and he will not have to fight against either of them."

Vice President Farias spoke up, "In this privilege of providing for the welfare of our young friend am I to have no voice? I will be glad to welcome him to our Military Academy and to my home."

"Thank you, gentlemen, but John already has a home with me. We will let him and his father decide between the Academy and the Mineria."

As the dignitaries left the room, President Santa Anna said, "Dona Inez is waiting to see you. My aid will show you to her rooms."

John was taken to the quarters of the president, furnished in French antiques and objects of art from the continent, for a visit with the first lady of Mexico. She was pretty, gentle and warm hearted. She explained that her husband admired John, wanted him to be part of their family and invited him to move from the archbishop's palace and live with them.

Dona Inez was born January 21, 1811. She had married Santa Anna in August, 1825, and was described by Wilfred H. Caldicott as "a woman of the coast, affectionate and simple in action, prompt and early about her duties in the morning dew and under the stars, with hands hardened by the milking of cows; clothes in cheap cloth with mind strong to manage majordomos or peons; often mounted on a side saddle in the style of the time on her favorite horse."[5]

Relieved of some of his fears, yet still apprehensive, John made his way from the Presidential Palace into the *Zocalo* and wandered through the market. Natives sold their produce under matting shelters set on tripods like huge umbrellas, with their wares spread on the ground: corn, tomatoes, peppers, leeks and artichokes, oranges, limes, mangos, bananas and plantain. Water carriers toted heavy jars fastened about their foreheads.

An Indian bore a crate of chickens on his back with a basket of eggs roped on top. A papoose dangled from the shoulder of a barefoot mother in a white cotton robe.

John wandered among the noisy crowd, feeling removed from it all. He recalled the president's eyes were strange and roving and hard to read. As for Dona Inez, he felt he could trust her. He made his way back to Archbishop Posada's palace. The next day, with the help of the friar, he moved his few possessions across the *Zocalo* to the presidential palace.[6]

10

Drawing of the Black Beans

*A*LTHOUGH JOHN HILL WAS SECURE in Mexico City he was deeply concerned about his brother Jeffrey who had been left in Mier with the wounded Texans and his father, Asa, who was part of the captive company traversing the wild and hostile country. When the prisoners left Matamoros for the south they were planning to stage a revolt.

The Mexican commission in charge of their feeding received from the government the sum of twenty-five cents per diem for subsistence of the prisoners. It was soon discovered that less than five cents a day was expended on a Texan. Spoiled sea bread had been laid in at Matamoros. The men rejected it with protests. Meager rations of the cheapest flour were then doled out. The two meals a day were made up of this low grade flour and refuse beef to be cooked as they could prepare it without utensils or provisions of firewood. The repulsive food, the harshness of the guards and the misery of their foot journey enraged the captives who rebelled against their betrayal at the hands of Santa Anna.

Captain Cameron organized a scheme to overcome the guards and make a get-away but his plans were misunderstood so the move was not attempted in Sacarte. They made the effort again at St. Catherine but the guards were vigilant and they failed. They decided to make a try for it at the Hacienda de Salado some 150 miles north of San Luis Potosi. Fisher and Green and their company, traveling a few days ahead of them, had learned of it. Fisher opposed the plan while Green encouraged it.[1]

Just before sunrise on February 11, 1843, as they were preparing to move, the Texans were to charge the guards. Captain Cameron raised his hat with a flourish and cried, "Well, boys, we will go it!" The Battle of the Rescue was underway.

He rushed for one of the sentinels at the inner door of the yard where they had been quartered for the night, while Sam Walker grappled with the other. Grabbing their rifles, they knocked them out and ran with other prisoners to tackle the 150 infantrymen on guard in the outer court. Surprised and bewildered by this early-morning revolt, the Mexicans gave up their guns and surrendered. The Texans grasped rifles and ammunition from the stores, crying, "They are at our mercy. But let's spare them and push on to the Red Caps."

These troops were on guard outside the hacienda. The prisoners opened fire on them and the Red Caps scattered and fled around the wall. The cavalry were forming and men mounting. The Texan fire caused them to whip up their animals and disappear. The prisoners now ran to the horses and mules that had been saddled for the morning journey and seized mounts for a dash into open country. They leaped into the saddle and joined the stampede toward the north. So began the revolt of 193 Texans. Eighteen were dead and wounded in the fray. Some felt they could not share in the breakaway and were left behind.

By darkness that night they reached the hacienda San Salvador where they fed their horses and slept a few hours. They rode twenty hours without water until they came to a *rancho*. A European whom they met urged them to keep to the main road but they decided to take to the mountains. At a brief council some said stick to the roads and push north. But there were others who reasoned that they would certainly be captured if they passed through the towns.

On February 15 they had been so long without water that they killed the fattest horses and mules, drank the blood, jerked the meat for food and set out on foot. Men wept as they stuck bowie knives into faithful beasts that looked at them with astonished eyes. Saddle flaps were used to make sandals for their feet.

The escapees became scattered. On February 18 Asa Hill found himself with Captain Cameron and a group of about fifty. Many were too weak to travel. Some were chewing and eating negro-head and prickly-pear leaves to produce moisture in their mouths, but these astringents greatly aggravated their sufferings; while others, with tongues so parched and swollen that they could not close their mouths, were scratching in the shade of bushes for cool earth to apply to their throats and stomachs.[2]

Seeing a column of smoke, they decided to advance no matter who might be there, hoping that water would be found. Several of them crawled over the parched earth after throwing away their rifles. The smoke came from the campfires of Mexican troops.

Captain Cameron surrendered his company, demanding and receiving a promise from Governor General Mexier that they would be treated as prisoners of war. During the next few days the Mexican troops led pathetic groups of Texans into their camp as they rounded them up, giving them scraps of beef to eat and dribbles of water. They were now tied together in pairs by rawhide thongs so they had to cook one handed and sleep fretfully side by side. The Mexicans stole their blankets, money and clothes so that they suffered from the bitter nights.

They were marched south as fast as their weakened condition permitted, housed at night in stock pens. Several were beaten with whips because they broke the rawhide thongs that bound them. The company had grown now to 160, with new derelicts being added each day to the tragic procession. Ten had died in the mountain and desert.[3]

On reaching San Salvador Asa had the thongs removed from the wrist that tied him to his companion and irons fastened on him, binding his left hand to the right hand of his mate in chains. The irons rubbed away the flesh and made the men's arms swell, turn black and cause intense suffering. When the dejected company reached San Luis Potosi the wife of the governor visited the Texans. She ordered the officer in charge to remove the shackles. He protested but at her insistence sent for a blacksmith who cut the chains away. The compassionate woman bathed the arms of those who were infected. This demonstration of kindness offset some of the cruelty that the captives had met among the Mexican people.[4]

William Stapp wrote of the condition of the Texans after their recapture: "When we arrived late in the evening at Pass Benido, where the enemy's infantry were stationed, our wasted and attentuated forms struck horror and compassion into the minds of all who saw us. No congregation of the newly-risen dead, who had been buried in the ragged serements of the pest house, could have inspired such mingled emotions of surprise and disgust as did our ghastly and tattered crew. All half-naked, some bare-footed and with an odd shoe and sandal-legs torn and lacerated by the rocks and brambles, our hair and beards bushy shading profiles cut down by hunger and suffering, to the pallid, pinched and sharpened expression of death, eyes sunk into the very beds of their sockets and sparkling with fitful light, half-frenzied, half-ferocious, inspired doubts with the beholder whether we came from the asylum or churchyard.[5]

Big Foot Wallace described his personal appearance: "As for myself, I had worn from necessity the same suit of clothes I had on when we made our escape from the guard and after traveling in them all this time over dusty roads and sleeping in them at night on the ground, it can be easily imagined my costume was not exactly suitable for a ballroom or a fashionable assembly. But little was left of my shirt, my hat had long since gone by the board and in its place my head was partially protected from the sun by a red cotton handkerchief wrapped around it like a Turkish turban.

Big Foot Wallace. (Courtesy Texas State Library.)

"I had but one shoe left which was in a very dilapidated condition and in lieu of the other, a rawhide sandal strapped on my foot with leather thongs. My coat was tattered and torn by thorns and, like Joseph's, from frequent mending with all sorts of materials, was of many colors. The remnant of my pantaloons hung upon me in shreds that were bound together by thongs or strings—add to this a countenance that had been guiltless of a thorough cleaning, I am ashamed to say how long.

"Such a beauty did I grow that if my old sweetheart, Jenny Foster, could have seen me her heart would have relented and she would have reversed the cruel decision which sent me packing off to Texas some years before."[6]

Bigfoot Wallace described the privations in their effort to escape. "We suffered horribly and could find no water and the cactus leaves that we chewed for their moisture made our tongues and lips swell; then we had to kill our horses for food and some of us drank the blood, trying to slake our terrible thirst. Some of the men died. The majority were recaptured by the Mexican military.

"I had been without water for five days. A Mexican soldier had a gallon gourd half full of water and he gave it to me to drink. One of the officers warned me not to drink too much at a time or it would kill me and tried to take the gourd away but as he was short and I was tall he could not reach it. I held it till I drained the last delicious drop. I fell to the ground and went to sleep. I slept a long time and woke up as good as new and proceeded to lunch on my dried mule."

The dismal procession reached Santiago April 26, four months after their surrender at Mier. Here they found the fire eaters, who had been imprisoned there when news of the Salado break was received. The boys were then marched on ahead to Mexico City.

The cavalry lined up around them, fresh troops in new uniforms, strict and vigilant in their supervision, having been impressed by reports of the treachery and ferocity of their prisoners.

Two weeks later the handcuffed Texans were marched back into the same hacienda courtyard in Salado from which they had fought their way out. Colonel Barragan and the Red Caps, whom they had spared as they took the horses for their get-away, were waiting to take their revenge. In a short time they heard the report: every tenth man was to be shot. Santa Anna had dug up an old law, classified them as brigands and ordered the executions. General Mexier would have nothing to do with the bloody business. Colonel Domingo Huerta had accepted the job, and the Red Cap company were to do the shooting.

Colonel Huerta called the muster roll and then announced, "The order from General Santa Anna states that one in each ten men is to be shot. So seventeen will be chosen by lot."

A Mexican officer crossed the courtyard carrying a small-necked pottery jar which he placed on the low wall before the Colonel. He poured into the jar 159 white beans and then scattered over the top seventeen black beans. He then covered the jar with a cloth.

"Every man who draws a black bean will be shot immediately," Colonel Huerta continued. "The

Drawing of the Black Beans painting by Frederick Remington. (Courtesy Museum of Fine Arts, Houston.)

officers will draw first. The men will then draw in alphabetical order. There is to be no exchanging of beans. If a man draws more than one bean and one is black, he must be shot."[7]

The company of prisoners waited before the officers and their Colonel below the low wall. Guards with rifles and bayonets lined the top of the outer hacienda ramparts. Outside the infantry and cavalry surrounded them in tight formation.

The Texans whispered among themselves. Captain Cameron broke the silence with, "Well, boys, we have to draw, let's be at it." He moved forward, manacled to Colonel William P. Morrow, who had watched the Mexican lay the black beans carefully on top in order to force the Texan officers to draw the death sentence.

As Cameron thrust his hand into the jar Morrow whispered, "Dip deep, captain."

Cameron pushed through toward the bottom of the jar and got a white bean. A Mexican took it and laid it on the stone wall. The faces of the officers around him registered disappointment. They wanted Cameron, who had become a symbol of Texan resistance. A ripple of gratitude swept through the prisoners.

With dignity and firmness they drew: Colonel William F. Wilson, Captain William Ryan, Quartermaster Judge F. M. Gibson and Captain William F. Eastland.

Bill Eastland, a Fayette County neighbor of the Hills, was the first to draw a black bean. His manacles were struck off. He was led to one side of the court where the doomed men were ordered to stand.

Eastland said, "I hope that my country will not seek to avenge my death. But for her own honor I implore her to never lay down her arms until her unconditional freedom has been secured and ample reparation made for these evils. I know that some have thought me timid, but thank God death has no terrors for me!"

The guards led him away and Asa moved up toward the fateful jar as his name was called. The black beans were by this time well scattered through the jar. He drew a white one.

He stopped to talk with Robert Beard, who lay on the stones of the yard. Robert was speaking with his brother William, who had brought him a cup of water. "Brother, if you get a black bean I will take your place. I want to die."[8]

William answered, "No, I will keep my own place. I am stronger and better able to die than you."

They both drew white, but died soon after from their bad treatment.

Some joked as they faced the jar, "Boys, this beats raffling all to pieces." "This is the tallest gambling scrape I was ever in." But soon all were solemn, even those who had drawn white.

When young James Torrey drew his black bean he said to a Mexican officer, "After the Battle of San Jacinto my family took one of your Mexican boy prisoners into our home as the Hill family did. We raised and educated him, and this is our reward."

Some 400 eyes were intent on J. M. N. Thompson who held his moment on the stage. He moved away from the jar with head bowed. By this time the Texans could sense what a man drew by the way he moved.

Happy-go-lucky Big Foot Wallace, one of the last to draw, figured that only about twelve beans were left in the jar and two of them were black. His chances were about five to one. He strode up and stuck his hand into the jar, fingering the beans. One felt larger than the others, so he hung onto the smaller. He tugged to pull his clenched fist through the jar neck. The Mexicans laughed when Big Foot opened his paw and they saw the white bean.

A local Roman Catholic priest was on hand to receive confessions, but the Texans ignored him. The priest approached Major Robert H. Dunham, asking if he wished to confess and receive the sacrament. The major answered tartly, "I confess not to man but to my God."

Luck was against Henry Whaling, one of Cameron's bravest men, who cried, "They don't make much of me anyhow, for I know I have killed twenty-five of the yellow bellies. At least they won't cheat me out of my dinner. Bring me my rations." He ate all the food that was carried to him, smoked a cigar and then was bound with cords to the other doomed men.[9]

The eyes of the condemned were bandaged and they were placed on a log near the wall with their backs to the executioners.

"Let us face you," they pleaded. "We are not afraid to look death in the face!" The Mexican colonel refused all requests and ordered the Red Caps to open fire. They blazed away for ten to twelve minutes, lacerating and mangling the bodies of the Texans. Henry Whaling was still living after fifteen bullets had penetrated his body. A soldier shoved a gun next to his head and blew his brains against the wall. One of the guards fainted at the sight of the brutality and was saved from falling over the parapet by fellow soldiers.

The main body of the Texans was separated from the bloody scene only by the stone wall. They heard the shots and cries as their friends were murdered.

The next morning they were marched on the road south past the unburied bodies. Some thirty days of painful traveling, cursed by their guards and weighted down by their chains, brought them near the capital.

They were crowded into a four-room building at Huehuetoca so close together that they could not lie down at the same time. There were no windows and oxygen was soon exhausted so that their candle went out. Their shouts for air were scorned by the guards. The Texans set to work with their knives to whittle a breathing hole in the floor and took turns lying down to inhale the air that came through.

This was the night when Captain Cameron was unchained from his partner and taken away. The men were fearful that he would not come back. In the morning as they washed at the cattle trough, they slipped stones into their pockets, ready to fight for his life.

"Where is the captain?" they asked. "He will be along shortly and join you," was the evasive reply.

As they marched south they halted at the sound of rifle fire. "Captain Cameron has been shot!" they cried bitterly.

Since the battle of Mier, Mexican leaders like General Canales had feared and disliked the popular

Scot. After the revolt at Salado he had been constant-ly under watch. Informed that he was to be executed, Cameron wrote a dignified letter of remonstrance to the British minister in Mexico City, criticizing the Mexicans for such treatment of a British subject. He was led outside the village. A priest asked him if he wished to make a confession. The Highlander answered "No. Throughout life I believe that I have lived an upright man and if I have to confess it shall be to my Maker." After tying his arms behind him the guards tried to bandage his eyes. "Tell them no!" he shouted. "Ewin Cameron can now, as he has often done before for the liberty of Texas, look death in the face without winking!"

"Fire!" he called out, giving his own order for the volley that ended his life.

The prisoners, with ragged *serapes* draped about them like cloaks over their tattered clothes, stumbled on toward the capital.[10]

After the black bean executions at Salado they had marched a distance of 500 miles. Several died under the privations. Robert H. Durham, having drawn a black bean, wrote his mother the following letter:

> Dear Mother:
>
> I write to you under the most awful feelings that a son ever addressed a mother, for in half an hour my doom will be finished on earth. I am doomed to die by the hands of the Mexicans for our late attempt to escape the orders of P. Santa Anna, that every tenth man should be shot. We drew lots. I was one of the unfortunate — Alas, I cannot say anything

more. I die, I hope with firmness. Farewell, may God bless you, and may He in this my last hour forgive and pardon all my sins. Farewell.

Your affectionate son,
R. H. Durham[11]

11

Grim Perote Prison

*D*URING THIS TORTUOUS JOURNEY of his father and fellow Texans John learned his way around the Presidential Palace, ate meals with *El Presidente* and Dona Inez, visited Mineria College and met General Tornel's sons, Augustin and Manuel, who were students there. He was invited to the Tornel's home and also to the home of Vice President Farias, who arranged for him to tour the Military Academy.

It was also John's good fortune to meet Ambassador Waddy Thompson, who served as American minister to Mexico. He poured out the story of the Mier prisoners and their abusive treatment and pled for intervention by the United States. He learned that the American was already working to gain release of the members of the Santa Fe Expedition who had been locked up in Perote Prison. He related his experiences with Ampudia and Santa Anna and asked the minister's advice on how to deal with the enigmatic Mexican president and his plan to adopt him and educate him.

Ambassador Thompson wrote in his *Recollections of Mexico*:

"Among the prisoners taken at Mier was a shrewd and handsome boy of about fourteen years of age, John Hill. On his arrival in Mexico this boy was not closely confined as the other prisoners were, and he came to see me and requested that I should ask the president to release him. I told him to go himself and I am sure that Santa Anna would be more apt to do it on his own application than on mine.

"A few days afterwards the little fellow returned to my house very handsomely dressed and told me that he had been liberated and gave me the following account of what had passed between him and the president. When he requested Santa Anna to release him, the latter replied 'Why, if I do you will come back and fight me again The Santa Fe prisoners were released on their parole on honor not to bear arms against Mexico and it was not three months before half of them had invaded my country again, and they tell me that you killed several of my Mexicans at Mier.

"The little fellow replied that he did not know how many he had killed but that he had fired fifteen or twenty times during the battle. 'Very well,' said Santa Anna. 'I will release you and what is more, I will adopt you as my son and educate and provide for you as such.'

"The boy was sent to the home of General Tornel, the Minister of War and was really as I know adopted on a full footing of equality in his family and treated with the most parental kindness. He was afterwards placed at the principal college in Mexico where he was pursuing his education when I left the country. General Santa Anna not only paid the charges of his education but in all respects cared for him as a son. Soon after his own discharge, little Hill came to me to request that I would obtain the release of his father. I told him no, that he was a more successful negotiator than I was, to go and try his own hand again. He did so and obtained at once the release of his father and afterwards of a brother, who was also among the prisoners."[1]

The young foreigner who had suddenly been brought into the inner circle of the Mexican government set out to glean all he could about the former arch enemy who now emerged as his sponsor and protector. The mercurial leader had entered the army as a cadet in 1810 when he was about sixteen. He joined the rebels during the revolution of 1821 and was soon a brigadier general. Following a rebellion in 1833 he was elected president as a liberal but soon turned to a conservative position. After his invasion of Texas in 1836, his defeat and capture at San Jacinto, he lost prestige and went into retirement. He recaptured his waning popularity after his encounter with the French during the brief Pastry War of 1838 and was made acting president the next year. With the overthrow of Bustamante he was inaugurated as chief executive October 7, 1841, in the cathedral by the light of countless candles. He was met at the door by Archbishop Manuel Posada, who presided over the Te Deum in his honor.[2]

Santa Anna was tall for a Mexican, about five feet ten inches, lithe and athletic in build. Ambassador Waddy Thompson spoke of him as a "finely proportioned person." Fanny Calderon, wife of the first Spanish ambassador to the republic of

Mexico, called on him at his Magna de Clavo estate, wrote of his attractive home there and stated that he was "a gentlemanly, good looking, quietly-dressed, rather melancholy-looking person, with one leg, apparently somewhat of an invalid and to us the most interesting person in the group."[3]

His eyes revealed astuteness and cunning and were a key to his complex personality. He was endowed with many gifts. He loved finery and luxury and collected art and antiquities. He was fond of statues of Napoleon and thought of himself as the Napoleon of the West. His harsh voice could be modulated to move and sway men through eloquent oratory. He was an organizer, whipping a motley mass of new conscripts into an army in short order. A soldier from the age of sixteen, he was a master strategist and a daring and cruel fighter.

He liked glittering uniforms with epaulets of silver and gold, ornate carriages and a retinue of dragoons, a sword set with gems, a saddle embossed with precious metals, and gold snuff boxes. He was fond of gambling, especially cock fighting, and amorous in his adventures with women. He was generous at times and passionately vicious at others.

He staged spectacles in the New Theatre, finished in 1843 and called the Santa Anna Theatre. It was said to be the finest in the world and comparable to San Carlos in Naples. It seated 7,000 to 8,000, with eight tiers of seats and splendid chandeliers. He was adept at handling the masses. His portraits were hung in public places and statues were erected in his honor.

The display of magnificence was viewed by the frontier lad who was suddenly thrust among the leading citizens of an imposing metropolis. He had lived in the Archbishop's Palace, been given a home in the Presidential Palace and taken into the warm circle of General Tornel's family. He had visited Mineria, the historic college founded in 1531. Its buildings of hewn stone and its distinguished professors of natural science, medicine and philosophy formed a contrast with humble and newly founded Rutersville College. When the scientist Humbolt visited Mexico City in 1804 he reported that the scientific institutions of the city were equal if not superior to those of the U.S.A.[4]

John mingled in the pulsating life of the plaza, which was fronted on the north with the cathedral and Archbishop's Palace, to the south of which lay the museum and market. To the east was the National Palace and on the west the Parian or public market, where every article of female dress in vogue among the people was kept on sale. Every interval of this square not occupied by these massive buildings was filled with arcades under which were small fancy stalls of flowers, books, cutlery and bijouterie, while above was the Mexican Palaise Royale of billiards and monte rooms. "The game of monte prevails like a monomania among the people. There are reputed to be 1,000 monte dens in the city."[5]

The streets were full of men in uniform. It was a country where the military were dominant. There were numerous Indians in evidence. "Some 4,000 Indians live in Mexico, many of them in mental degradation and religious superstition, their lives as yet untouched by the revolution. They plodded through the street hawking their vegetables, fruits and merchandise."[6]

The National Palace of Mexico. (Courtesy University of Texas at Austin.)

John shared afternoon rides in the presidential carriage in the Paseo where he saw a cavalcade of carriages and horsemen attired in fashionable dress. Waddy Thompson wrote of this spectacle: "Nothing is regarded more vulgar than to be seen on horseback in a dress coat or any other than a roundabout. These are richly embroidered with silk or with gold and silver lace and covered all over with buttons. Their cherivalles are equally fine and generally open from the knee down. More elaborate still were the saddles and bridles of the horses with their masses of hand-wrought silver. The price of such equestrian furnishings alone frequently ranged as high as a thousand dollars, while five thousand was not unheard of."[7]

The gentry and the military in an array of fine garments and jewels gathered for soirees and balls, while the peons labored and the *mendigos* and *ladrones* pilfered the shops and pled for alms.

Ambassador Waddy Thompson had arrived in Mexico City in April, 1842. He recorded that the night after his coming the streets were filled with a procession of dignitaries of the church. The archbishop led the solemn crowd of more than 20,000 representing the church, army and government. Santa Anna's wife, Dona Inez, was reported to be dangerously ill and the last rites were administered to her while the vast throng prayed for her. Thompson wrote that "she was spoken of by everyone, even the bitterest enemies of her husband, as a lady of rare virtue, and with the benevolence which belongs to the character of women everywhere. She had strenuously exerted all her influence with her husband for the release of the Texas prisoners."[8]

The petitions of the people prevailed and she recovered. She was moved by this experience and felt that God had spared her to help others. The story of her survival increased her popularity.

Santa Anna was devoted to Dona Inez, who exerted an influence for good upon him. Yet while he was in Texas during his invasion of 1836, he staged an illegal mock marriage with a San Antonio girl. After his defeat in San Jacinto he had her sent back to Mexico and set up in a house in Jalapa.

El Presidente liked privacy and comfort. He left the city as often as possible, delegating authority to his associates in order to relax amid the peace of his estates. Magna de Clavo was his favorite. John visited this *hacienda*, enjoyed its gardens and explored the countryside.

John had been informed by the gatemen at the Presidential Palace, who comforted him in his anxiety over his father, that reports indicated the Texan captives would arrive in the near future. A few days later there was a commotion in the streets. Spectators trailed a small unit of Mexican soldiers who guarded what looked like a group of *ladrones* who were barefooted and in rags. John discovered that they were the four fire eaters from whom he had long been separated. He made his way to them and called out their names.

The boys did not recognize him in his Spanish attire and could scarcely believe that he was living in the Presidential Palace as the adopted son of Santa Anna. John heard from them the story of the revolt at Salado, the recapture of the Texans, the drawing of the black beans and the execution of the seventeen, followed by the shooting of Captain Cameron. Five had been killed during the Salado revolt; ten had died or been lost in the mountains after the break for freedom. The fire eaters on their separate march south had maintained some contact with the other Texans and they told John they believed his father was alive and that he should reach the capital before long.

John interceded with *El Presidente* on behalf of these youthful captives. Santa Anna asked for their names. When Orlando Phelps was mentioned, the president repeated the name Phelps, stating that when he had been held captive on the Brazos River at Orizabo he had stayed in the home of a Dr. Phelps who was a surgeon in the Texas army. During a period of despondency he had taken poison and tried to end his life. Dr. Phelps saved him by pumping out his stomach. Could this boy be his son?

John assured him that he was. Santa Anna sent for Orlando and told him that he was to stay in the palace with John. He ordered his tailor to outfit him with clothes and promised to take care of him and see that he was returned safely to his father.

John and Orlando visited Billie Reese, who was sick in the Hospital de Jesus Nazarene. Billie was the largest of the boy musketeers. General Thomas Green had said of these brave lads, "Had our 261 men at Mier been boys, I do not entertain a doubt but that I should have been spared the pain of recording their captivity, sufferings and deaths."[9]

John called on the American Minister, Waddy Thompson, to whom he had gone several times for counsel regarding Santa Anna's proposal to adopt him. He asked him to intercede with the president and seek the release of Billie Reese. He prevailed upon him to visit the sick boy and hear the story of what had transpired since the Battle of Mier.

Waddy Thompson took a fancy to Billie and promised to seek an audience with Santa Anna. When he arranged for the two boys to see *El Presidente*, John requested freedom for his young friend. Billie jeopardized his chances when he stated that he did not want to be sent home, that he wished to go to Perote Prison and take the place of his brother, Captain Charles Reese. He explained that his brother was engaged to be married and had to get back to Texas.

Santa Anna pointed out that Billie had just recovered from a long illness and was in no condition to face imprisonment in Perote. He had a chance to go free; he should take it.

Billie then asked for permission to visit Perote and see his brother enroute to Vera Cruz, and this request was granted.

As Santa Anna looked out from eyes that were haunted by a cynical mistrust of the world, he commented to Waddy Thompson that he was a fool to liberate the Texans, that they would probably come back again to fight against him. Whereupon Billie affirmed boldly that he would. Later, during the Mexican American War, he was among the forces that took Mexico City.

John was buoyed up by the hope that his father would soon appear. The palace guard promised to send him word when the next contingent was reported to be nearby. Some time after the arrival of the fire eaters he saw a file of men lurch down a street toward the plaza, surrounded by armed infantrymen. He hurried forward to scrutinize their haggard faces as they clumped along on flopping and broken sandals.

The column was ordered to halt and a group of Mexicans carrying chains started to fasten their manacles to the legs of their prisoners. John elbowed his way through a gathering crowd. He recognized his father, bearded and exhausted. As a blacksmith circled a chain about Asa's ankle, John protested vehemently, announcing that he lived in the palace and demanded in the name of Santa Anna that his father should not be bound. Asa Hill was as amazed as the guard to see John in Spanish clothes, announcing that he lived with the president of Mexico. He watched the boy run toward the palace.

John found *El Presidente* and informed him that his father had arrived looking like a ghost, that heartless men were chaining him and reminded him of his promise. Santa Anna assured him that he would permit no harm to come to Asa, ordered him freed from his manacles and sent to the Hospital de Jesus Nazareno for medical care. He was invited to come to the palace to talk about John's future as soon as he was able.[10]

John made daily trips to the hospital carrying food and flowers. Señora Santa Anna had her cook prepare soup and other delicate dishes to help build up the strength of the prisoner. John found opportunity to relate his dramatic story and to hear details about the journey Asa had shared with the Texans.

As Asa recovered he was outfitted in new clothes and received by the president who explained his admiration for John and his desire to keep him in school in Mexico and provide him with the best possible training. He explained that the boy had turned down military education at Chapultepec but had started studies at Mineria College.

Asa Hill made it clear that he did not wish John to become a Mexican citizen, but remain a Texan and keep close to his family and his people. He could sense the advantages of studying in Mexico City but urged that John should be free to make his own decisions as to his future.

He was assured by Santa Anna that the boy would be encouraged to preserve his ties with his family and would be at liberty to go back any time. He stated that everything in his power would be done to equip him for a happy and useful life. He promised that he would arrange for Asa's transportation home and do the same for Jeffrey when he was brought to the capital.

On April 26, 1843, the final Texan equipage had reached a stopping point near Mexico City where they were quartered in an old convent and assigned to repair the roadways around Santa Anna's estate at Tacubaya. As reward for the 1,000-mile march over a four-month period, the Texans were outfitted with official prison clothing. William Stapp wrote: "To each man was presented a jacket and trousers of coarse flannel, with longitudinal stripes of alternate red and green running up and down, a coarse domestic shirt with sandals to match, completed with turnpike regimentals and roars of laughter and many a jest shook the old corridors of the prison as we were accoutered in the motley gear. When fully equipped, it would have puzzled Shakespeare's fantastic moralizer, the witty Lucio, to decide whether our dress bespoke the foppery of freedom or the morality of imprisonment."[11]

Americans, English and other foreigners in the area brought them clothing. They were told by the authorities that the Mexican government was too poor to support prisoners unless they labored, and that all must go to work. Although required to undertake dirty jobs, they were fettered with heavy chains weighing from eight to ten pounds each.[12] Equipped with wooden shovels of the rudest manufacture, with crowbars, picks and grain sacks, they were escorted by a strong body of cavalry early each morning to nearby Tacubaya. Crowds of *lazaroni* and half-naked men and women followed, cheering them as they crept along chained in pairs. The ankle chains were suspended from an iron hook fastened to heavy belt.

The prisoners chuckled at themselves in their grotesque striped garb, at their primitive tools as they tried to make light of their miserable breakfast of *tola*, which they used to wash down four ounces of bread. The noon meal consisted of boiled beef and five ounces of bread. At night they were given boiled beans.

They were moved from the convent into a group of dilapidated buildings which were an improvement over the dismal quarters they had shared with criminals. They were furnished with rush mats spread on the brick floor for beds, sleeping without blankets or any kind of covers.

Tacubaya became the scene of their hard labor. Founded by the Aztecs in 1270, it had developed into a fashionable suburb. Santa Anna's residence there was a "large two-story stone edifice built in the prevailing

Texan prisoners repairing roadway at the Palace of Archbishop Manuel Posada. (Courtesy Texas State Library.)

fashion of the country, situated on a gentle eminence. The prisoners marched from their road-building project at this country place about a half mile, bearing their sacks which they filled with sand and stone and carried them back to the villa while others dug up the ground with crowbars, leveled it with wooden shovels and then laid a pavement of stone.[13]

The president and Dona Inez took John with them in their carriage on trips to the Tacubaya villa. He mingled with the prisoners, talking with old friends, listening to the reports of their hardships. He was grateful that his father had been spared this heavy labor.

Upset by the inconsiderate treatment of the Texans, he complained to his excellency and Dona Inez. His foster mother endeavored to alleviate their lot and requested their discharge, but Santa Anna stubbornly refused.

The Texans were adept at delaying tactics and at work stoppage. They boasted that they graded only one hundred yards of the roadway during two months time and accomplished less work than a pair of Irishmen would have achieved in one week.

In order to hurry up the project and humiliate the independent prisoners, the guards hitched some of the strongest men to wagons. One day Big Foot Wallace seized a cart, neighed like a horse and galloped down the steep roadway. Guards shouted at him to halt but his momentum kept him hurtling along. When he reached a curve he broke free from the traces and let the cart crash on down the hill, where it was wrecked. He waited for the Mexicans to recapture him, expecting to be punished. But they laughed at the escapade along with his fellow captives.[14]

Although they often succeeded in outwitting the easy-going guards, they berated Santa Anna, who kept himself secluded from their hostile eyes.

When the dictator passed them in a coach drawn by six mules, surrounded by a cavalry guard, he bowed stiffly as if to say, I am enjoying my revenge upon you barbarians.

His prisoners remarked that when he was their captive in Texas he was lodged in a pleasant cottage on Galveston Island, sent to Washington and entertained in Dr. Phelps' country home and not forced to pound stone. Their clowning and stalling irritated their captors, who duly informed his excellency. After four months Santa Anna grew weary of the wiles of the Texans and their efforts to escape and ordered them to be moved to the ancient Castle of Perote, the most dreaded and impregnable prison in the nation.

They set out on foot, traveling via St. Martin over the tablelands of Puebla some 6,000 feet above the sea among some of the most fertile fields in Mexico, where wheat, maize, maguey and fruit flourished. They passed through beautiful Puebla and continued some 96 miles east to Perote through a wild moorland plain intersected by mountains, through adobe villages and a sandy country covered with light powdery dust.[15]

The Castle of Perote, built in 1770, was located southeast of Mexico City at the foot of the mountains known as the Coffer of Perote. The prisoners reached the mighty fortress on September 21.

It was described by William Stapp, one of their company:

"This formidable keep is built of stone, quadrangular in form, and having projecting horns running out at each angle, 150 feet long and about sixty feet broad. It embraced an area of twenty-six acres surrounded by walls thirty feet high, fourteen feet thick at the base and ten feet at the top. The walls are enclosed by a moat sixty feet wide and ten feet deep crossed by a drawbridge to the east connected with a ponderous gate, the only entrance or outlet to the castle. A range of prison cells, eighteen by thirty feet in depth and surrounded by an inclined terrace reaching to within six feet of the top, runs around the entire circuit of the interior walls. The cells are lofty and arched, being lighted by grated windows above massive wooden doors and floored with tough cement ten inches deep.

"The center of the enclosure is occupied by a double square court, an acre in extent, surrounded by tiers of two-story buildings, the upper stories of three sides of the inner tier being used as officers' quarters, whilst the western side contains the chapel and governor's quarters. The lower or basement store is occupied as barracks and the exterior buildings used variously as workshops, storerooms, armories, granaries and stables. In the northeast and southwest horns are the powder magazines, the other two being appropriated at the time as lumber houses. Sixty-four pieces of ordinance, of nine and six pound caliber, were mounted on the terraces above the prison cells, and some brass pieces of large and small dimensions with several howitzers lay about the castle."[16]

The Texans, calloused by countless hardships, took stock of their new incarceration. The bare floors of the cells were their couches with one blanket to every tenth man. The mountain air was cool and chill winds blew through the gratings of the dungeons. They we chained and locked up every night until they were released at nine A.M. They were compelled to wear chains at all times except when they were ill.

Thomas Jefferson Green testified that the lightest of the chains weighed about twenty pounds. The manacles were called "jewelry" by the captives. Various ingenious devices were developed to release these fetters at night in order to momentarily escape their harassment. When they were unexpectedly inspected they would quickly snap the irons back on.[17]

Food was miserable. They were forced to forage and supplement their diet with what they could buy from peddlers and to cook over open fires.

Every morning a party of a dozen or so of the captives was paraded with an overseer, who carried a cudgel in his hand. Each man was handed a bunch of evergreen twigs tied around the end of a stick about four feet in length. With these crude brooms they cleaned up the square of the castle, followed by others with wheel barrows and shovels who picked up the refuse and garbage.[18]

What galled the prisoners most was the rule that they must doff their hats when they passed General Jarero, the governor. They usually ignored the order and received a blow from his cane. One of the most degrading forms of punishment was being forced to pull loaded carts, yoked like oxen, carrying stone some four miles along a mountain trail. Sometimes the Mexican officers forced them to draw their captors in carts through the town of Perote.[19]

12

The Incorrigible Texans

FOLLOWING JOHN'S APPEAL to the American ambassador General Thompson on behalf of Billie Reese and the resulting audience with Santa Anna, the president arranged for Billie's journey to Vera Cruz where he would take ship for New Orleans. John was allowed to accompany him as far as Perote where Billie visited his brother.

They reached the prison after a ride of 160 miles. It lay in a narrow valley some 8,000 feet above sea level. The mighty wall of the formidable fortress was sixty feet high, built of volcanic pumice stone. No one had ever escaped from this impregnable prison.

After they passed the guard house the drawbridge was lowered and their horses clattered over the moat, up the steep way into the grim plaza that was set about by the prison barracks. They were given a warm welcome by their old friends who told them how they were locked up every evening in their cells, showed them the ankle chains and the fake irons they had created to slip on in place of the fetters to fool the guards. The cells were damp and cold. There had been numerous epidemics and twenty-two prisoners had died. A number of the men had been sick with "jail fever." Big Foot Wallace had been so delirious that he was called the *mucho grande loco Americano*.[1]

The boys were entertained by the prisoner pastime of louse racing. A cowhide was spread on the stone floor. A circle was drawn on the hide and inside it a smaller one and at its center a cross. Men entered their favorite lice in the competition, the point being that the first one to reach the cross in the center won the stakes. They gathered around, intent on the movements of the body lice, cheering and groaning according to their luck.

Card playing was another pastime for whiling away the weary hours. A number of crude violins had been fashioned. They sang songs of the homeland and even danced when their energy was whipped up by Mexican wine.

The visitors heard stories about Captain Gozeman, known as Old Guts, who was in charge of their rations. Prisoners were theoretically allotted twenty-five cents a day for food, but Old Guts handled the funds, spent about eight cents on each man and pocketed the rest. In the morning he gave them a pint of *stolla* (corn gruel) sweetened with a pinch of sugar. At dinner they received a pint of soup, sometimes beans, a few ounces of gluey beef, spoiled most of the time, with a six-ounce loaf of brown bread. Supper was a second edition of breakfast. Once in a while they picked up a little cash for performing extra prison work and managed to buy coffee, sugar and *burra* milk, a piece of meat or a few vegetables.

The Texans had become quite proficient at cooking whatever food that came to hand. Sailing

Master Lyon browned coffee beans and ground them on a flat stone. Dan Henrie nursed a fire with an Indian fan while he sang "Long, Long Ago" and "The Soldier's Tear." Colonel Fisher hashed the beef while Lieutenant Clark peeled potatoes and mangled peppers. General Green cut up onions and mixed the condiments. Charlie Reese stood over the fire, stirring the *burra* milk that had been mixed with water, coffee, eggs and sugar, watching it carefully to keep it from scorching. General Green, after frequent tastings, pronounced his approval and all hands agreed that this was the best dish they had yet cooked. The hot drink was ladled out with the stew. There were compliments on the unusually agreeable diet of the day and references made to rat soup which had been eaten in times of scarcity. Several of them boasted of being the most expert rat hunters in Mexico.

A farewell party was staged in honor of the fire eater Billie Reese, who was toasted in *mascal* wine and loaded with letters to be carried home.

Ambassador Waddy Thompson, as he returned to the U.S.A., paid a visit to the Texans. He had already interceded with Santa Anna on behalf of the Bexar prisoners who had preceded the Mier men to Perote. He prevailed upon Santa Anna to release the thirty-six who had been captured by General Woll and carried away. This gesture of generosity by *El Presidente* was accompanied by an outburst of abuse against the Mier men. William Stapp recorded the desolation felt by his comrades:

"Thompson expressed the deepest sympathy in our misfortunes, but besides confirming the reported armistice between Texas and Mexico, could furnish no further information regarding our destinies. No provision in reference to us had been so much as alluded to in the armistice and no efforts that he was appraised of, open or secret, were being made by our country for the amelioration of our lot. Deserted and abandoned by those to whom alone we were entitled to look for sympathy and succor, our fortitude did not desert us but, nerved for the worst, we thanked the generous American for his successful exertions on behalf of our more fortunate comrades and bade him adieu."[2]

Waddy Thompson wrote of the Mier men: "I do not believe that the rank and file of any army was ever superior to the Texan prisoners in courage and other high qualities."[3]

The Texans had hoped vainly as special days came near, such as the president's birthday or some festive period, that their release would be ordered, but there was no confidence in their captor, as Stapp stated: "He is the imperious, unsympathetic embodiment of action and authority, with an exorbitant ambition and love of power, a monster of perfidy and hypocrisy—a vindictive tyrant, at one time the country's benefactor and at another, its scourge."

Thomas J. Green wrote voluminous protests to his captor. He felt that Santa Anna held a special dislike for him since he had personally witnessed the president's cowardice in June, 1836 following the Battle of San Jacinto when he was captive of the Texans aboard the *Invincible* and was terrified to face the people on the shore of the Brazos River. Green wrote President John Tyler of the United States April 25, 1844, requesting American intervention on behalf of the prisoners.

John wondered why Santa Anna kept saying no to the Texans. He was puzzled by the man who continually sought to protect him but was brutal to his friends. How could he be gentle to Dona Inez and kind to him, but harsh to the Mier men? He confided to Dona Inez, who did what she could to alleviate the suffering of the prisoners.

Thomas J. Green spoke warmly of John's character and his devotion to the Texan cause. William Stapp wrote, "Through the partiality John is said to enjoy with the usurper (Santa Anna) his brother and father were likewise successfully released and money provided them to reach home. He frequently visited us in our confinement, expressing the keenest solicitude for our welfare and the more earnest hopes of our speedy deliverance. This is the boy whom the newspaper accounts of the Battle of Mier represent to have killed seventeen Mexicans. He behaved with the gallantry of a veteran throughout the bloody fight and we dare say, from the deliberation and frequency of his shots, must have added largely to the enemy's loss."[4]

During one of John's visits at Perote he learned of an audacious plan of escape that was being considered. For weeks the carefully concealed strategy continued as shifts dug through the dense wall with chisels they had smuggled from the workshops, sometimes prying off as little as a hatful a day. The chips were carried out under their blankets and dumped in the *comun*. By the first day of July they reached the outside of the wall which was still protected by a shell of stone. A supply of blankets, coffee, bacon and chocolate was accumulated through bartering with Old Guts. Sixteen finally determined to make the effort, including Tom Green, Dan Henrie and Charles Reese.

On the night of the attempted break Green left a letter for Santa Anna to be delivered by Colonel Fisher. Fisher spoke his farewell to the sixteen: "As you have determined upon the hazard, though the chances are greatly against you, God grant that you may reach home in safety. I know you will do us justice and will be of infinitely more service to us there than here." The men were to creep out their hole and down the high wall on ropes they had brought in from the village and spliced together, then climb over the outer wall, cross the moat and the high fence to freedom. They waited tensely for darkness.[5]

At six o'clock the turnkey locked the doors and the bugles sounded in the plaza. It was a dark night with cold rain falling. The men, hidden under their blankets, cracked jokes to cover up the anxiety. In order to get the sentinel outside the door in the right mood, they passed him eggshells full of *mascal* wine through the iron grating until he grew sleepy. Some played a game of *monte* with little squares of soap, handing a few chunks to the sentinel so he would join in the gambling and not hear the noise of the escape. Another group joined in a dance, singing and clapping their hands.

At seven o'clock the first man went to breach the hole, but it was too small for him to pass through. Two hours of desperate work were required to enlarge it. At nine the Irishman, John Toowig, slipped down the rope. By half-past twelve all sixteen were at the foot of the wall in the moat. Over the wall and the fence they made their way to freedom, off on foot for the seacoast. With map and compass they took to the mountains and broke into two parties.

Most of the remaining Texans did not sleep well but turned on the cold stones, aching with worry. They wanted to delay in every way possible the discovery of the break. At nine o'clock Old Guts and the guard came to prison quarters with the order, "*A formen! A formen!*" The men made excuses for not forming in line and stayed inside.

"Old Guts stormed at their tardiness," wrote General Green. He went into their cells in person to look where the absent were and found them not; he inquired of the balance. One says, 'They are at the *comun.*' Another says, 'They are at the *tienda.*' These places were sent to but they were not to be found. Our boys said among themselves, 'We will put them off to the last minute so they can get the deeper into the mountains.'

"During this time Guts swelled and raved. 'Where are they?' he thundered out to the interpreter. When some of them said, 'Well, it is no use to put it off any longer, let him have it,' Van replied, '*Deiz y seis falten*'—sixteen deficient. 'Where are they gone to and how did they get out?' bawled Guts in a still louder tone. '*Quien sabe?*'—who knows? was the reply. They commenced the greatest possible row: the whole castle was alarmed—officers and soldiers turned out; the governor came forth with death-like horror upon his countenance; officers and guards flew all over the castle, examined every nook and corner, the top walls, went around the great moat—but still did not discover the breach, the hole having been so carefully stopped with a blanket. The last place where they thought of looking was in the prison cells, and after much useless search one of the officers pulled back the small shutter in the center room which covered the loophole and found to his inexpressible horror, our breach obliquing to the left. 'Who could have thought these daring Texans would have undertaken such a task? They surely are kin to the devil. This castle has stood these hundred years and no one ever dared such a thing before.'"⁶

Colonel Fisher handed the governor the farewell letter that General Green had written to Santa Anna which stated that none of the Mexicans had cooperated with them in the escape and no one should be charged with neglect of duty. The general made his final thrust at the president: "Not having been trusted upon my parole, which neither the love of life nor fear of death could have induced me to forfeit and the climate of Perote not suiting my health, I shall for the present retire to one in Texas more congenial to my feeling."⁷

The governor in his panic dispatched the letter to Santa Anna by a special courier who was ordered to ride day and night before the president got word of the escape. He forgot to order the cavalry to set out in pursuit until more than an hour had passed. They tracked the Texans to the point where they had separated the night before but could follow them no farther. The troops broke into small units and set out along the road and rugged passes. These delays gave additional time to the prisoners who pushed ahead as rapidly as possible.

The sixteen escapees of July 2, 1844, toiled on

over the mountain roadways. Their prison sandals were soon worn through and their feet bruised and bleeding. One-half made their way, after heroic exertion, to freedom. The other eight were captured and put under double irons and extra guards at Perote. Fortunately the other eight, including General Green, Captain Reese and Dan Henrie and five Bexar prisoners fell into the hands of a friendly Mexican who placed them under the care of a group of robbers who guided them by night to Vera Cruz. Here they took ship for Texas.

The Perote break pleased John Hill as it angered the president. John was gratified when Santa Anna carried out his promise to return fire eater Orlando Phelps to his home in Brazoria County. When John's brother, Jeffrey Hill, came through the capital Santa Anna promptly made arrangements to send him by way of Perote to Vera Cruz and a homebound ship. Jeffrey had left Perote Castle on May 19, 1843, loaded with mail to be carried to Texas. While in Vera Cruz the young man was arrested and held in prison. Through the instrumentality of the American counsel he was liberated and finally succeeded in making arrangements with a sea captain who took him to the U.S.A.[8]

Asa Hill also set forth under an escort to Vera Cruz after he had partially recovered from his extreme hardships. The president provided for his steamship travel to New Orleans and then to Matagorda. Asa died in Rutersville, Texas, in 1844, soon after he was reunited with his family. He was buried in Cedar Creek next to his oldest son, Dr. Green Washington, who passed away a few weeks before his father.

John was responsible for the safe return of Billie Reese, Orlando Phelps, Jeffrey Hill and Asa Hill and was a supporter and helper of the other prisoners. On one of his trips to Perote he heard of the dramatic story of the second escape that rivaled its predecessor of July 2.

After the first escape the guards checked the men a dozen times a day, came into their cells and poked around at the walls with minute care, not thinking it possible that there could be any other mode of escape "In this they were much mistaken. During that terrible malady of hard work and starvation which swept off so many of our men, the governor granted the survivors permission to cover their pavement floor with heavy boards, being softer to sleep upon than stones. They then conceived the plan of sinking a perpendicular shaft through the pavement of their floor some forty feet deep and tunneling underneath the main wall so as to reach the bottom of the great moat upon the outside. Tremendous an undertaking as this was, these bold men completed it in forty nights, for they could not work upon it in the daytime."

The morning following their second break, "the remainder of the prisoners, who looked upon it as another triumph of Texan prowess, did not wait for the guards to find it out, but ran to Guts and said that 'another sixteen of the Texans have gone, *señor*.'

"'*Hai Dios! Diez y seis falten? Carajo!*'—'My God! Sixteen missing! Oh villains!' was his first exclamation but at the thought of the gloomy dungeons of San Juan de Ulloa which stared him in the face, he burst forth into a roaring cry. The tears rolled swiftly down his fat face and fell upon his still fatter belly, which labored like a bellows, to the no small amusement of the Republicans who well nigh split theirs with laughter. Had Heraclitus been a prisoner, one peep at Guts would have made him laugh.

"The whole castle was instantly in an uproar. The governor came around to assure himself of a work which all said the devil had a hand in. When he saw it, he exclaimed, '*Mucho trabajo*'—'much work,' and consoled himself by saying that 'They had a professional engineer to conduct it.'"[9]

Nine of the sixteen reached their homes safely. Seven were recaptured. The prisoners who remained were treated with increased repression and cruelty. A letter arrived from General Green announcing that he was back in Texas and that the Texas Congress had appropriated funds for relief of the men in Perote. This aid never came but the report did afford them momentary hope that they had not been completely abandoned.

Ambassador Waddy Thompson of the U.S.A., on his visit to Perote, confirmed a reported armistice between Mexico and Texas but could furnish them with no other information. No provision referring to the prisoners had been so much as alluded to in the armistice and no efforts that he could discover were being made to better their lot.

Appeals were made to Santa Anna by General Jackson, Henry Clay, John Calhoun and other prominent Americans but he resisted their entreaties for clemency. He is reported to have planned liberation of the Perote prisoners before they made their prison break. When he heard that report, he lit a cigar with the paper on which the order had been written, saying, "This is the way I will liberate them!"

Wilson Shannon was made the new American minister to Mexico. He arrived in the summer of 1844 and paid a visit to Perote on his way to the capital. He went into every cell and talked to the men. He pledged that he would make a vigorous effort to get them back to the U.S.A. This statement tended to quicken their lagging hopes. His first official note to *El Presidente* asked for their liberation.

Santa Anna replied, "I have the honor to inform you that, as well for the efforts made on various occasions by the members of Congress of the United States, as through respect for Messrs. Jackson, Thompson, Clay and others of respectability, I have liberated many of the Texan prisoners who were captured in various actions and encounters between the Mexican army and the adventurers, and now only those are retained in prison who, abusing the kindness extended them, have attempted to escape by assassinating the Mexican soldiers who guarded them. These criminals deserved death and nothing but the *mildness and magnanimity natural to the Mexican character* has prevented its application. Justice, however, demands that they should be treated with greater severity than those who have not aggravated their faults by stabbing the innocent soldiers who guarded them. This is all I ought to reply to your esteemed communication, and in having the honor to do so, l have the satisfaction of subscribing myself, for the first time, your most affectionate, attentive and constant servant, Antonio Lopez de Santa Anna."[10]

William P. Stapp lived two months near Perote

after his release and returned to visit his former prison mates. He stated that "he found them in low spirits. Description would fail to elaborate the misery depicted in their emaciated appearance and their despondency, hopeless looks and tones. A more rigorous discipline and refined cruelty had been adopted towards them since I left as to excite their surmises that the government had instructed the authorities to push them to some act of desperation as would justify their general massacre.

"Several had been attacked and beaten. For more than a month their rations had been reduced to the lowest standard of supply, the little allowed them being musty rice and rotten potatoes with meats of doubtful character and repugnant in flavor as to be only palatable to men reduced to the extremities of hunger."[11]

Ambassador Shannon did not forget the Perote prisoners following his arrival in Mexico City or after Santa Anna's irate refusal to grant their release. He wrote to the Texans, urging them to "be patient and wait a while longer." In a few days after they received the letter the joyous news came announcing their liberation.

On September 16, 1844, as they were lined up for inspection and roll call in the courtyard, it was announced that the oath of parole was to be administered, which would bind them not to take up arms again against the Mexican government. The oath was taken and signed by the surprised captives. Each man was given a passport by Old Guts which advised the citizenry to treat them with consideration.

The governor of the castle, "representing the

'magnanimous nation' and acting under instructions 'natural to Mexican magnanimity', gave each of the Texans one dollar to bear his expenses to Texas, being a distance less than 2,000 miles, and then turned them upon the open common as if they had been so many herbivorous animals. One hundred twenty was the aggregate number released, of whom there were at Perote 105, Vera Cruz 10, Mexico 3 and Matamoros 2."

At five P.M. the Mier men formed rank for the last time while the Mexican troops paraded in full dress uniform. The half-starved prisoners were turned loose in the valley with no provisions for their trip except their munificent gift of one dollar.

As they left the castle gates the battery gun opened in a parting salute. For nearly twelve months and twenty days they had been locked inside this fortress and for more than two years had been absent from their homes in Texas.

Big Foot Wallace wrote of one hardship they encountered along the way: "A few miles from Jalapa we were stopped by a company of robbers on horseback, eleven in number, who demanded our money. We told them that we had been prisoners a long time, had just been liberated and were not flush with money. They asked if we were Texans and if we had passports. I handed them mine signed by Santa Anna. They said Santa Anna was a scoundrel and wanted to know why the Texans didn't kill him while they had him. I told them that if I had had the keeping of him he would not have troubled Mexico any more.

"They offered to keep us company to Vera Cruz and protect us from further molestation. Night came on, they turned off the main road and conducted us to a large ranch or hacienda that appeared to be a sort of rendezvous for gentlemen of their profession. When the robbers entered, the people in the house exclaimed, 'How are you, Colonel? How are you, Major?' and other like expressions.

"Here an excellent supper was served and we were cordially invited to partake of it. A variety of fruit and excellent wine was placed on the table. I asked the robber chief if that was their usual style of living, and when he replied that it was, I told him if there was a vacancy in the corps I should like to enlist. This pleased the robbers and they drank the health of the 'gringo' in a full bumper. The next morning they filled our haversacks with provisions, gave us a half dollar apiece, escorted us back to the road and bade us *adios* with many expressions of good will."

The Mier remnants tramped into Vera Cruz, footsore and exhausted. They found a schooner, the *Creole*, that carried them to New Orleans in thirteen days. Yellow fever raged aboard the ship but they managed to survive due in large measure to the kindness of Captain Dessechi. When he learned what they had suffered at the hands of the Mexicans he refused to charge them for their voyage.[12]

13

Fall of Santa Anna

A BOUT A MONTH BEFORE the departure of the prisoners from Perote their benefactor, Dona Inez
Santa Anna, died on August 23, 1844. A massive
funeral service was held in the cathedral conducted
by Archbishop Posada with music by choir and band.
John Hill was among the mourners. He had lost the
mainstay of his security in the palace.

William Stapp spoke for the Mier men who
respected her as heartily as they disliked her husband, "The lady of Santa Anna, by universal testimo-
ny, deserved herself to be canonized, being renowned
for all the virtues and humanities that adorn the most
chaste and elevated standards of female worth. Over
the relentless selfishness of her husband she is reputed to have enjoyed no ordinary supremacy, mitigat-
ing the rigor of his resentments, and saving him from
the commission of numberless atrocities by the influence of her benevolent counsel.

"She was held in the affectionate regard of the
Mexican people and consecrated in the esteem and
gratitude of all the unfortunate, whom her tireless
charities aided and relieved."[1]

On October 3 *El Presidente* took a step that cost him the ill will of his people when he married by proxy a fifteen year old girl, Maria Dolores Tosta. The populace was displeased with this lack of respect for his much loved first lady. Due to internal disorders in the country and resulting political upheavals the honeymoon was interrupted. He was taken prisoner and placed for a brief time in Perote Castle, where he had gloated over the Texans who had caused him so much grief. He was shipped to Havana June 3, 1845, with his girl bride on the first of his numerous exiles. Popular demonstrations led to the removal of his honored leg lost in the Pastry War, from public display and to its unceremonious discard.[2]

James K. Polk, who advocated bringing Texas into the union, was elected president of the U.S.A. in 1844. Congress took action and the Lone Star Republic was given this invitation.

The United States, as well as France and Great Britain, had many financial claims against the Mexican government. President Polk was anxious to purchase the Mexican territory as far west as the Pacific now that Texas had come into the union. He sent a representative to Mexico City but leaders there were afraid to even talk with him. They wanted to recover Texas, and its annexation was considered a cause for war. Polk prepared for what appeared to be inevitable conflict. He appointed General Zachary Taylor head of the army in the Southwest.

A base was established on the Gulf opposite Matamoros. General Pedro de Ampudia warned Taylor to disband and return to the Nueces River but the Americans replied by building Ft. Texas. Ampudia's successor, General Mariano Arista, crossed the Rio Grande and killed eleven American troops. Old Rough-and-Ready Taylor reported to President Polk, who asked Congress to declare war. They responded in the affirmative on May 13, 1846.[3]

President Polk had sent a representative to Havana to talk with Santa Anna, stating that the U.S.A. did not want war and would pay generously for any land it appropriated. Santa Anna in exile made proposals regarding his cooperation and what he would expect in return. He slipped back to one of his estates and waited to be recalled to lead the fight against the *Yanquis*. When the call came he was ready with fiery proclamations and fund-raising enterprises. He set to work with vigor to equip the army.[4]

The people John knew at the National Palace and Mineria College were bitter against the Americans over their declaration of war.

John Hill witnessed the chaos and confusion in the city as the American forces drew closer. The Battle of Molino de Rey near the capital was a bloody engagement. The young military cadets fought bravely to protect their military academy at Chapultepec but were defeated. Santa Anna was forced to resign as president and as head of the army. There was no national government.

John was present when the American forces took over the capital on September 14, 1847. He served as an interpreter and aided the Americans and the Mexicans. He persuaded the high command to remove the occupation forces who had taken over Mineria College. His efforts helped in some measure to restore order at the college and in the city. A number of old friends showed up. Billie Reese, back again as Santa Anna had prophesied, along with Captain Charlie Reese, Gilbert Brush, Big Foot Wallace, Johnnie McMullen and Dan Henri Drake. The exuberant Dan Henri was captured once again by the Mexicans but managed to stage a spectacular escape, running away from a company of the enemy in full daylight to reach his associates in safety, just in time to join in an attack against his captors.

These comrades in defeat made good their vow to return and square accounts with their conquerors who had failed to keep their word. John considered returning to Texas when the troops departed but decided that he would first complete his education.

Asa Collingsworth Hill, John's brother, served as a captain of a spy company with the American forces and initiated his contact with Mexico which was to continue through the years.

Captain Jack Hays of the Texas Rangers came with the American forces. He received permission from General Winfield Scott to capture Santa Anna. Hays and his men pursued him as he fled from Mexico City. They reached his quarters at Tehucan immediately after he had stolen away toward Vera Cruz. They found the trunks and luggage that he had abandoned. The men opened them and gazed at his ornate garments and the gowns of his young wife.[5]

When Hays caught up with the elusive prey he found that the charmer was being wined and dined by his American conquerors. The *Yanquis* were so chivalrous in their treatment of their defeated enemy that Hays had to drop his plan to seize and imprison the resourceful schemer who had made so much trouble for his neighbors to the north. The dictator managed to reach the coast and then Jamaica by April 8, 1848, moving on to Cartagena, Colombia in the spring of 1850, where he bought an estate at Turbaco.[6]

He was recalled and inaugurated as president April 20, 1853, the year of the Gadsen Purchase. He endeavored to put down a rebellion in the south and another in the west but had to flee Mexico City August 9, 1855, after he had been defeated by his liberal opponent, Benito Juarez. He left with one hundred trunks and twelve servants.

William Stapp described the efforts of the president to dazzle his subjects:

"Fifty hussars dash in five abreast followed by a coach flashing with gold and crimson and drawn by four bloods driven by a coachman in gorgeous livery. An equal number of hussars in similar order follow in the rear of the coach while on either side, caracole, three aide-de-camps, caparisoned, man and horse in the most splendid style. The coach and its escort move slowly around the enclosure and as it passes every hat is off and fans are moved in salutation. The object of their homage is a military dignitary, dressed in a uniform of blue and gold, and blazing with medals and diamond decorations. His arms are folded on his bosom, a la Napoleon, and he nods his head in haughty acknowledgment. It is Don Antonio Lopez de Santa Anna.[7]

During his third exile he lived in Colombia and St Thomas, returning after the collapse of the regime of the Emperor Maximilian. He journeyed to New York to engage in efforts to overthrow Maximilian but

GRAL. D.ⁿ JOSÉ MARIA TORNEL.

Ministro de la Guerra en Enero de 1835 hasta Abril de 1837, por segunda vez de Obre. de 1838 á Agosto de 1839; por tercera de Ocl.ᵉ de 1841 á Junio de 1844; de Febrero á Julio de 1856 y por último de Abril á 8bre. de 1853. Estuvo al frente del Ministerio de Relaciones de Febrero á Marzo de 1839 y dirijió la Hacienda en Julio del mismo año.

General Jose Marie Tormel.
(Courtesy University of Texas at Austin.)

he failed. On his return from New York to Vera Cruz he was arrested and exiled to Cuba.

He made his way from his fourth exile to Mexico City for the last time March 7, 1874, his fortune spent, his estates sold, his eyesight failing. On this visit there was no pomp or fanfare. Citizens no longer rallied about him. His wife had become embittered. His children provided him with some support as he lived in a humble house, unrecognized and unhonored. He died June 21, 1876, during the presidency of Porfirio Diaz and was buried in the cemetery of the village of Guadalupe.[8]

John was saddened by the fate of this unfathomable man. He was grateful for the protection and privilege he had received and the support and affection of Dona Inez.

But the Tornels had given him a home more like his own. He had the companionship of their two sons near his age who were in the same college. Santa Anna had given his consent to this third adoption.

The first to adopt John was General Pedro d' Ampudia who kept up a correspondence with John as long as he lived, continuing to address him as "my dear son." He was in charge of a division of troops in the north during the war with the U.S.A. Defeated there in 1846, he served under Santa Anna until his fall in 1854, then retired to his *hacienda*, La Soledad, in the state of San Luis Potosi. In 1862 he joined the forces who supported execution of the emperor. He was arrested as a supporter of the reactionary regime and sentenced to be shot. John heard the report and visited the prison where the general was confined. He possessed sufficient political influence with the new president to secure the liberation of his friend.

Asa Collinsworth Hill, brother of John, wrote from Mexico to William Webb October 2, 1867, regarding a visit he had made with John upon General Ampudia:

> Brother and I have just returned from a visit to General Pedro Ampudia, who is in prison for serving the imperials and he says he never served them an hour in his life, which is true. He is sick in bed. Of the many things he related to me, one caused tears to flow. He talked of father (Asa Hill) and brother Jeffrey, and expressed a desire to see all the relatives. Pointing to brother John, he said, "There is my grandson. He is a good boy. He told General Santa Anna to put him into prison but to release his father and brother."
>
> I could not help but shed tears when I left him on his bed of affliction, near unto death.
>
> I would be glad if you would write a letter of petition of the proper authorities for his release. They say every now and then he will be released, but there is no telling, they work so very slow in this country.[9]

General Ampudia was returned to his villa where he died August 7, 1868, and was buried in the Pantheon de San Fernando.

John Christopher Columbus Hill as a young man in Mexico City. (Courtesy Texas State Library.)

14

Engineer, Entrepreneur, Physician

*D*URING THE TUMULTOUS TIMES that swirled around his guardian, John Hill was busy at Mineria College perfecting his Spanish and carrying on his courses of study. In his second year he was made chairman of his dormitory. He enjoyed the companionship of Augustin and Manuel Tornel.

There were periodic visits to explore historic sights and field trips in geology and mining.

There were colonies of Americans and English and Europeans in Mexico City, generally involved in business or diplomatic service.

John met a charming English girl, Mary Murray. They became devoted friends. Mary had been reared by strict Victorian parents. Her mother had recently died of yellow fever and her father was unduly solicitous of his daughter's welfare and deportment.[1]

The romance blossomed into love and John called frequently at her home and also met her at the home of their mutual American friends. Her father became alarmed when the report was circulated that the couple were planning a secret marriage. He talked with Mary, who denied the rumor.

Her father assured her that while he believed her and at the same time had the highest regard for her lover, he had decided a temporary separation was the better course. When John had completed his education and was settled in business or other profession, he would most willingly give his consent. Mary pled with her father but to no avail.

Hurried preparations were made for the immediate embarkation of the family on one of the vessels which was then in readiness to sail from Juan Blas to California and which had been chartered by Mr. Murray to convey his manufactured goods to that state where he also had a home. His two daughters and son were accompanied on their voyage by a friend, Mrs. Tiernay and her daughter. In two months the father removed his effects to the "Golden Gate" where he thereafter resided.

In the meantime young Hill continued to write his sweetheart, although she dared not reply. Finally her father said, "I will reply to all these letters myself," which he did although she never knew what he wrote.

She did not receive any more letters but heard through some source that John had embarked on a certain vessel for California, which vessel she afterward knew to have been wrecked and therefore believed him dead.

In the course of time she met a very worthy gentleman by the name of Masterson. But before marrying him she acknowledged that her heart had been given to another whom she believed to be dead.

She recounted to him (and afterwards to her four children) all the circumstances connected with her early love.

Though she married without love, as many do, when she came to recognize all the many excellent attributes of mind and heart her husband possessed, and he had become the father of her children, she learned to love him and they lived happily together.

(This story was written in 1898 by Lucy Hill, John C. C. Hill's favorite niece.)

John Hill graduated in 1850 from Mineria College, trained in civil and mining engineering. He continued graduate studies at the University of Mexico and also served as a tutor of English at Mineria.

He was appointed a mining engineer at the famous San Miguel and Regla silver and gold mines. Here he sensed the vast potential of natural resources in his adopted country and the need for economic development.[2]

While working in this area he met and married Augustina Sagredo of Real del Norte, daughter of General Sagredo, a Spaniard and the brother of Raymon Sagredo, one of the foremost artists of the Pelegrin Clave school of painters.

John and Augustina visited Santa Anna when he was in residence at the National Palace and at his estates. Their views on the needs of Mexico varied. John was for reform: education of the people, lifting the standards of living through development of mines, railroads and land. He traveled widely through the country. He was criticized, threatened and attacked by landlords, mine owners and politicians because of his efforts on behalf of the peasants.

He was called *"pano de lagrimas,"*—"one who wipes away tears," by the poor.

Four children were born to John and Augustina Hill. Angelito died in 1856 when he was not quite one year of age. Maclovia was born November 15, 1856. She married Alfredo Dawe who was of English parentage. Alberto was born in 1863 and Carlos in 1867.[3]

John Hill made frequent journeys to Texas and the States and kept in close touch with his kinfolks. A number of his letters which have been preserved portray him as a warm-hearted person who was devoted to his large and colorful family.[4]

He made himself an intimate part of Mexican life, yet he remained an American citizen and never severed ties with his homeland. Albert M. Gilliam in *Travels Over the Table Lands and Cordiollos of Mexico*, tells of a visit with Hill, mentioning that he spoke only Spanish. This was a false observation. Although Hill identified with his foster country and spoke its language like a native, he never ceased using English.

Benito Juarez, the reformer, opposed Santa Anna and led a second revolution as he came to power. He was a marked contrast in his simplicity and his demand for a republican form of government, freedom of religious beliefs, surrender of land by the church, free public schools and individual rights. He was bitterly opposed by the church as he led a struggle for the oppressed.

Conservative forces set up the Archduke Maximilian of Austria as emperor with the aid of Napoleon III. The emperor was overthrown and shot. Juarez became president again July 15, 1857, stating, "the people and government must respect the rights of all." He started building railroads and schools and struggling to solve the financial morass. John Hill gave his support to these endeavors.

Juarez was reelected in 1867 and in 1871, but progress was slow because the country was ravaged by civil strife.[4a]

Jose Perfirio Diaz broke with Benito Juarez and seized power in 1876. He was a revolutionary who was diverted from reform through compromise. He was reelected for an eighth term in September, 1910, perpetuating himself in power for nearly thirty-five years. He set out to promote industry and business, to build railroads and harbors, to suppress banditry and establish the rule of law. But the Indians were held down for the benefit of the hacienda owners. Diaz developed into a conservative. He permitted a hacienda economy that held the peons under the rule of the *haciendado* and the church.[5]

He did, with the help of John Hill and others, bring some material progress. In 1876 there were only 691 kilometers of railroads, in 1910 there were 24,717. There was one bank in 1876; in 1910, thirty-two. In 1876 there were 7,500 schools; in 1910 there were 12,500. In 1876 there were some $50,000,000 in United States investments in the country; in 1910 there was an increase to $1,000,000,000.

In opposition to Santa Anna's conservatism and dictatorial politics, John Hill sympathized with Juarez and Diaz. He made it clear that he loved Mexico and her people. He worked to promote the welfare of her citizens and to develop neighborly relations with the United States of America.

Hill refused to submit a claim against the Mexican government while investigating suits made by Americans and Mexicans. When he was charged by a Mexican newspaper of seeking such financial remuneration for himself, he stated in the press that this was false and that he would always depend upon Mexico to do him justice. He said that he had received an education from the country and would consider himself ungrateful, although a citizen of the U.S.A., to appeal to the commission to establish any claim against the Mexican government.

John was actively involved in the mining industry, largely in lead, zinc, coal and silver. Mexico possessed mineral riches. He organized new mines, working for the industry and investing personally. He wrote to his brother-in-law William Webb from Talancingo on September 4, 1881:

> Your views on mining business are perfectly correct; and I am satisfied that there is no undertaking so profitable at present for us both as this kind of occupation; but it would require a little capital to commence with, say two or three thousand dollars to defray expenses at home while we would be essaying in traveling from one mine district to another, in different parts of this Republic. Nothing but the want of sufficient means keeps me at home; I would be willing to start tomorrow on such a scheme as you propose, for I know we would never have to regret such an undertaking. By profession I am a mining engineer, and assayer, and having everything necessary, we

could ourselves ascertain the true lay of all the ores, and know at once their true value. I will have occasion to write to you again on this subject.

All join me in love to you, sister Sarah, and to each one of our relatives in that city, with many kisses for each one of the children.

Fraternally and affect. your brother—
John Hill[6]

* * * * *

Olivia Mine in
Santa Rosalla, Coahuila
November 20, 1896

My ever dearest Niece Lucy:

I left Monterey on the 11th inst—with Mr. Mealy; we first had urgent business to attend to in Monclova at the Mining Agency, and then we returned to Bajan on the Mex. Intl. from where we came out to these mines in the Santa Rosalia range of mountains where we have located five different mining properties of which only two (Olivia & Tolteca) are being opened up. So far they promise to be productive in good lead and silver ores, but up to the present we have only taken out about twenty tons that will very near produce enough to cover expenses, with hopes of increasing a sufficient quantity to leave a fair profit—I have, free of all expenses, a ten per cent interest in all these mining properties, so if any one of them should turn out a *bonanza* you can depend upon your share; just the same as the interest you shall have in the 500 shares I represent in the "Mina de Agua" negotiation at Cerraloo (or Cerrabo), which will soon begin to pay dividends—I will inform you more particularly about this last enterprise on my return to Monterey, early next week.

—Uncle John[7]

* * * * *

John wrote Lucy June 6, 1893:

Dear Lucy,

Judge Galindo is expected tomorrow night from the City of Mexico and will only stop over one day before proceeding to Durango. On his arrival there he will let me know when I will be needed, so, in the meantime I will remain here and complete the arrangements for taking possession of a new mine in this district and have the title deeds perfecto.

I also have a commission to sell between four and five hundred thousand acres of land in the Laguina District Coals. Metcalfe and Crook are my Agts. They are now dealing with an English syndicate and confidentially believe they will purchase the estate (Las Delicias) if they will only send a competent committee to investigate the property. Of course I will be ready to go and show them everything whenever they come. This will not interfere in the least with the main object I have in view, "that grand enterprise in Durango".

I frequently find myself so lonesome that I feel as if I was compelled to write to you and keep myself from getting the *blues*. (His wife had died in 1891.) The hope of making a little fortune is the only thing that could take me so far away from my loved ones. On such occasions, the only pleasure I expect to enjoy is to receive letters from you every few days. Please keep this in mind Lucy and write oftener. When you and sister write to any of the absent loved ones, please don't forget to give them my love.

I also wish to be remembered to all the Hill Colony in Austin including of course bro. George, sister Serena, Mr. Thompson's family and all the relatives and friends in your lovely city.

Your loving and most devoted—
Uncle John[8]

John's mammoth sale of land apparently succeeded He wrote November 12, 1894, to Lucy Hill from Eagle Pass

This morning I visited the coal mines at Sabina where I am to carry out the commission with the Soledad estate. The plans were approved.

Your loving Uncle[9]

John was a man of property. When he returned to Texas in 1880 he wrote from Fayetteville on November 2 to William Webb, his lawyer brother-in-law, stating that Cousin John Hill had offered $300 for two hundred acres of prairie land and 150 acres of timbered land in Wise County.

They agreed that the price was fair and the deed was prepared.

Monterey, Mexico
December 27, 1896

Dearest good Niece Lucy:

Today being Sunday I will certainly find time to write you a letter and tell you how busy I have been during this past week. Last Sunday night two hours before the train left I received a telegram from Mr. Flynn saying, "Please return by first train"—I only had time to take my supper, pack my valise and rush to the Mas. Nat. Station and got there only one minute before the train left. I got *here* Tuesday morning early.

I have been as busy as a bee, signing the *shares* of three mining companies as secretary in one, and in the other two as secretary and treasurer, for which I got two unassessable shares in each negotiation, besides my regular salary from the Flynns. The names of these mining companies are "Aztec," "Carbonate" and "La Plata" all near this city. Now, as to the "Mina de Aqua," in Cerraloo, where I own 500 shares, already paid for, I am glad to inform you that the concentrating works are in splendid condition, turning out several tons of lead and zinc daily; the lead is sent here to the smelters and the zinc is shipped to Germany where they pay the best price—most likely in January or February next we will commence to receive dividends.

I hope you got a registered letter I sent you from Eagle Pass with a Xmas gift. I was in hopes that your New Year's present would be from our Cerraloo Mina de Agua which is in bonanza from all accounts, but the Board of Directors, of which I am one of the members and inspector of the Co. besides, have not had time to visit our interests and find out the true standing of everything.

Now what I think is best of all, is the interest I represent in the mines Mr. Wm. H. Mealy is working near Bajan, in the State of Coahuila. The recent discoveries are certainly very encouraging. The quality and quantity of the one discovered right from the surface exceeds anything this side of Sierra Mojada. Next month we will commence shipping ore to the smelters in this city, and we will soon know the practical result. For good luck you shall participate of the very first dividends.

Remember me to each and all the dear relatives, most especially to the home folks (Bro. and sister).

As ever your most affectionate—
Uncle John[10]

* * * * *

John Hill worked as a civil engineer in railroad building as well as in mining. He constructed the railroad from Tampico to Tuxpan and the road from Piedgras Negras south into Mexico. His letters between 1876 and 1884 refer to the difficulties he faced in railroad engineering. His brother, A. C. Hill, worked with him on some of these rail projects.

Asa Collingsworth Hill wrote from Oakville, Liveoak County, Texas, on November 21, 1880, to his brother John:

> The R.R. from Corpus to Laredo via San Diego is going ahead. Some distance beyond San Diego will be the first R.R. of our state to reach the Rio Grande. You would see much to interest you to go the overland route. I am very busy but I will meet you at any point you may designate should you give me a few days notice in advance of the time to bring you to Oakville.
>
> Be sure to bring Carlos with you. Love to mother and all.
>
> Your very unworthy brother of the far Western Wilds—
> A. C. Hill[11]

Asa Collingsworth Hill wrote June 7, 1886, from Eagle Pass, Maverick County, Texas, on the border of Mexico to his brother-in-law, General William G. Webb at Albany, Shackford County, Texas:

Dear Bro. Wm.

Brother John is flying up and down the roads almost like a bird of the air. He returned Saturday from Saltillo (south of Monterey), and out this morning for Castanio, the present terminus of this road, and will return Thursday. Before he left, he read me a letter he had just received from you. We are quite sorry to learn of your affliction. We both believe that it is best for you to come as soon as possible to the City of San Antonio for I am sure the climate of the southern part of this state Coahuila, (Mexico) would put you up just right in a very short time—Monclova or San Bueno Ventura and spend a part of your time at those valuable springs Las Hernanas, Santa Catrudas or the San Lucas, all in less than a day's journey from each other. And my dear Brother William should you need any assistance that I can render just command me.

I wish you were now here and able to start with us on our trip to Saltillio and Laredo on right of way business. Be sure to bring that sweet little boy of yours with you, Eugene Blanton.

Now is the time for him to commence to learn the Spanish language.

A. C. Hill[12]

This letter, written to Sue's aunt, Willie Simmons in 1901, is typical of many that John wrote to his ever-widening circle of relatives, in his fine

Spencerian penmanship and with the same loving concern:

> Monterey N. Leon
> Mexico
> September 13, 1901

Mrs. Willie H. Simmons
Huron - Hill Co. Texas

My Dear Great Niece:

Your dear good letter of the 2nd inst. was sure enough a surprise but I am glad to say it was a very agreeable one, and as a proof of face I take great pleasure in answering it. As soon as my ordinary business affairs will allow me the time, I will try and give a brief account of myself to comply with your wishes, which are perfectly natural and legitimate in every respect, because they originate from a noble sentiment you have inherited from your parents.

Yes I do remember your dear good papa who was named after my oldest brother—Dr. Green Washington Hill, his father whom I saw the last time in 1842 at La Grange just before my father, brother Jeffrey and I started to join the Somervell expedition that was then being organized to oppose and drive back the Mexican Army under General Adrian Woll, who had just invaded Texas and captured the city of San Antonia.

At the time I was equipped for this

expedition by brother James Monroe who was one of the San Jacinto heroes and is now living in Austin, Texas. He made me a present of a fine little rifle and said to me, "Bro. John, this is not to be surrendered." I was certainly proud of my little gun and could never forget bros.' words.

When we all reached San Antonio 800 strong General Woll did not wait to give battle but retreated to the Rio Grande taking with him a good many of the most influential persons of San Antonio. General Houston ordered Somervell to follow the Mexican Army clear across the border into Mexico and chastise their audacity. General Woll got out of our reach, and Somervell at Larado decided to return to San Antonio with 500 men and the other 300 under Col. Fisher and Gen. Green went down the Rio Grande as far as Mier where we encountered the Mexican Army 3,000 strong under their Gen. in Chief Pedro de Ampudia, who had his headquarters in Matamoros de Tamanlipas. The battle commenced about 2 p.m. on the 24th of Dec., 1842 and lasted 23 hours. We surrendered to Ampudia on the 25th day of December, Xmas day.

Then all my comrades were surrendering their arms. I saw some curb stones close by which gave me an opportunity to break my rifle and throw it away. I was immediately taken before the General in Chief to explain my conduct, but fortunately it did not seem to displease General Ampudia, because I was kept at his Headquarters and allowed to see my father in the prison and my wounded brother in the hospital as often as I pleased.

From this date the history of my eventful life in Mexico commences. A little later on you will hear something of it through others that have undertaken the task.

Your very affectionate Great Uncle—
John C. C. Hill[13]

John Christopher Columbus Hill with his daughter Maclovia and her two daughters. (Hill family records.)

15

The Hill Family Saga

*J*OHN CHRISTOPHER COLUMBUS HILL cherished ties with his family, although he lived in Mexico. He was devoted to his wife and children and at the same time maintained close bonds with his kinfolks in Texas, making continuous trips back and forth and writing letters in lively correspondence through the years.

A sizable collection of his correspondence has been preserved. He wrote often to his mother, brothers and sisters, and to his favorite niece, Lucy Hill, and to his brother-in-law, General William Webb.

He invited his relatives to Mexico and enjoyed showing them places of beauty and interest. He traveled widely for a man of his times, pioneering in the development of a backward nation, building railroads, prospecting for minerals and opening new mines. His search for investors took him to New York, Chicago and to California. He reported to his associates in Mexico and his relatives in Texas. He wrote of the wild back country where he served as a mining engineer, stockholder, treasurer or trustee.

On March 17, 1881, John's daughter, Maclovia, wrote to her grandmother, Elizabeth Hill, in Spanish:

> My Adored Grandmother,
>
> I have the pleasure to send you many kisses from mother and myself and manifest the immense pleasure I have that they are building the railroad and we will have the pleasure of seeing you here more and more. Since the temperature is moderate, it could be very advantageous to you.
>
> Mother and I are wondering what kind of fruits you should like and the tamales we will happily make. How happy we will be then having you here with us.
>
> Please give to all my uncles and cousins many expressions of affection and you receive many kisses and the heart of your grand-daughter who adores you.
>
> Maclovia Hill[1]

The following letter was written by John to his daughter Maclovia, whom he calls Cova, on January 12, 1900. She was in Austin with her daughters, Maria and Angelina, who were in school there.

> My Dear Daughter Cova,
>
> I am taking advantage of this opportunity to send you a check from New York in name of your cousins "Hill and Hill" for the amount of $25 in gold, which can be cashed without difficulty at the First National Bank in Austin.

In my previous letter I asked if you wanted me to send you some money at a later time. I don't think you will get mad at me if I am sending you $25 in gold now without first having received your answer.

I suppose that you as well as the girls are taking two drops of Sulphuma every day before breakfast in 1/4 glass of water as a preventative for all kinds of illnesses, especially for intermittent fever and eruptions, and it also cleans the complexion thoroughly. You won't have difficulty in having the girls take it regularly. When the weather is very hot one becomes bilious and the sulphuma has the advantage of regulating the secretion of the bile and prevents constipation and headaches.

As the check is in the name of Hill and Hill you will not have to co-sign it.

Regards to Lucy and your uncles and kisses to you and the girls. Your father—
J. C. C. Hill[2]

Maclovia's daughter, Angelina, wrote to her cousin Lucy Hill (also in Spanish):

January 1, 1905

Dearest Cousin,

Since I received your dear letter with the five pesos you sent for my Saint day, I wanted to answer you, but we were moving to another house. Now I have nothing to do and will write you. On my Saint day I received many things. You gave me five pesos. Marie gave me a fan and one of my friends a little bottle of essence and a friend gave me a robe and many other things.

For Christmas I received many things and now for New Year I received two baskets of flowers from a man that comes to see me.

Mrs. Steele has a little baby girl. She is pretty and fat and is called Bessie.

Maria and I have had typhoid but now we are well.

Give all my cousins many kisses for me. Your loving cousin,

Adeline Dow[3]

John's Protestant heritage bred an independent spirit. Although he married a Spanish Roman Catholic he did not desert his church built and operated by the people with freedom to worship according to conscience.

When only a teen-ager he possessed the courage to stand before a supreme pontiff of the Roman Catholic hierarchy, the Archbishop Posada, who delivered the ultimatum that unless he was baptized by the one and only church, he would be damned.

John's niece, Delia Kerr, wrote January 15, 1880, from a visit with John at Tulamingo:

I went to the Catholic church the Sunday after I got here with all the family. Uncle John stood at the door and waited until his wife, daughters and Carlos got through with saying their prayers and crossing themselves.

I took my seat and watched the people, the way they worshipped God. I tried but could not pray there, no matter how hard I would try. So last Sunday I was feeling badly and did not care to go. Anyway, the park in this place is very pretty and I go there walking sometimes in the evenings.[4]

John's letters revealed deep interest in the practice of medicine.

His oldest brother, Dr. Green Washington Hill, studied medicine in Georgia and practiced in Texas. John mentions physicians he knew and corresponded with and one he helped find a place to practice in Mexico. No doubt he studied with some of these men as lawyers did with more experienced attorneys. He was often referred to as Dr. Hill. He mentions his valise, his medical bag, and refers to his patients. On returning home he often found them waiting for him. In his letters he continually expresses concern for the health of his relatives.

The Hill clan was a microcosm in itself—a little society. They shared pleasures and adversity and gave mutual support to one another.

John was an articulate letter writer, fluent in phrases of affection—darling, beloved, dearest and precious. He sent kisses to his "bouquet" of little nieces. He wrote his numerous letters with a steel pen dipped in ink, in straight, unwavering lines in the Spencerian script. He always used his special signature framed in a series of flourishing circles.

He wrote to his brother-in-law, General William Webb from Talancingo, September 4, 1881:

You could hardly imagine how glad I was to learn the good effect the waters from the Waukesha springs has had on you. There can be no doubt but that it was a stone that you passed from your bladder the day before you left Waukesha to return home, and it is really a great pity that you did not preserve the specimen, for it would have been now an easy matter to treat your case so very effectually after once knowing the composition of the calculi that originate in the kidneys. The most common of these formations are either uric acid, urate of ammonia, phosphate and oxalate of lime, or a mixture of the uric acid and oxalate of lime.

Your brother, John.[5]

In a letter to Lucy Hill December 10, 1882, John wrote:

Tell my dear good sister Jane I received her precious letter that I read over and over at night as I am so lonesome in this mining country. All of your sweet letters are my best company in my solitude. When I write to you I think I am also writing to sister Jane and my dear brother—as l have no time to make reference to any previous letters.

I am just delighted with the idea of your visit, and I hope you will enjoy yourself while here. If you wish to bring your little gun along there is lots of game.

Your Uncle John[6]

John wrote Lucy Hill from the Olivia mine, Santa Rosalie Coahuila, November 2, 1896:

> Tell sister Jane to let me know in time before she runs short of the antiseptic solution so that I can keep her supplied. Also tell brother that I have another pumice stone when he wears out the one I gave him for his corns. I wish he was here with Mr. Mealy to help him kill some of these fine fat deer, as he is so fond of hunting—we hardly ever ride out without seeing half a dozen.
>
> Much love to each and all the dear loved ones. As ever, your devoted—Uncle John.[7]

Dr. Hill, as he was called, wrote William Webb March 23, 1880:

Dear Brother:

> I prefer sending my own remedy for my sweet little Fannie, as I think it more reliable than any that could be had in Houston. One of the best among new remedies for Fannie is Eupatorium purpureum, third attenuation, six or eight drops in half a glass of water, after well incorporated. Give a spoonful from 4 to 6 times a day, decreasing the dose as she improves.
>
> The principal drugstore in Galveston has received right lately from Boerike and Tafel of Philadelphia a supply of Flomcopathic medicines. If you write to Capt. Walker he can get it for you; if not, your favorite doctor in

Houston can supply you with it. The common name of this plant is Queen of the Meadow.

Much love from all to sister. Most affectionately, your brother—
John[8]

John wrote September 27, 1880, of his concern for the health of his sister Bettie. Jeffrey had taken her for treatment at the mineral springs near La Grange, but she did not improve. When Dr. Hill heard this he wrote, "Tell her again and again that I am more than willing to go where she is and stay with her and doctor her as long as she wants me."[9]

The Hill-Webb-Kerr clan were active Methodists. At a convention held at Rutersville College the record states that one-third of the hundred and fifty delegates were from these three families. It was a convivial gathering day with chicken, roasting ears, cakes and pies and rousing hymns from John and Charles Wesley.

James Monroe Hill married Lucy Kerr, daughter of Hugh and Lucy Kerr, and lived forty-nine years in Fayetteville where their house may stand. They had nine children including Lucy Amelia, who became John's favorite niece, his correspondent and biographer. All the Hill-Webb-Kerr clan had large families. Lucy married Bird Jones. James Monroe died two days before John Christopher Columbus. The family held back the sad news from John C. C.

William Webb married Sarah Ann Amelia Hill. He planned to study law at Yale University but when Dr Green Washington Hill, his brother-in-law, died, he was asked to serve as guardian of his sister's children. He studied and practiced law in Texas. He was editor and publisher of the *Houston Telegram*. He was commissioned as a general by Sam Houston. General Webb and John C. C. Hill were devoted friends and steady correspondents.

Serena Pinkney Hill married George A. Kerr. Louisiana Elizabeth Hill married William Penn Kerr.

The Kerr, Hill and Webb children all attended Rutersville College.

The Blantons were also members of the Hill-Webb-Kerr clan. Thomas Lindsay Blanton, born October 25, 1872, the son of Thomas Lindsay and Eugenia Webb Blanton, graduated from the University of Texas in 1897, practiced law, became a judge and a member of the U. S. Congress, establishing his home in Albany, Texas. There were five Blanton children, including Joseph E. Blanton, rancher and scholar, who lives on the old homestead ranch. He knew scores of the Fayette County clan personally and has been a prominent figure in their activities. His father's sister, Annie Webb Blanton, his noted aunt, was a Ph.D. from Cornell. She was a stellar figure in Texas education, serving in many state offices and on the national level as a pioneer in public education and women's rights.

Houston Wade, a leading historian of this period, wrote my wife, Sue, January 27, 1924, from Houston:

"The Wade family were neighbors of the Hill family and we all lived around La Grange and Fayetteville in Fayette County. My grandfather was William W. Wade and my

great grandfather was David Wade. I have
often heard my people speak of the Nuckols
family and the Hill families who lived in the
same area."

Longtime neighbors and friends of the Hills,
the Thompsons had come from the same area in
Georgia as the Hills. They were of the same English
and Scottish descent. Thompson was a farmer and lay
Methodist preacher. He was active in the college and
community. He performed marriages for local cou-
ples. One of his sons died in the Mier expedition. The
Thompsons were neighbors of the Hills.[10]

One can only imagine the anguish that
Elizabeth Barksdale Hill endured through those long
months that Asa, Jeffrey and John suffered at the
hands of their barbarous captors.

Asa's homecoming was a heart-rending experience for Elizabeth Hill. To hear him recount the
details of the continuous pain and hunger of the long
marches, to embrace his frail and tortured body, must
have been a devastating tribulation.

From this ordeal he never recovered. He died
in 1844 soon after his return. He was laid to rest at
Cedar Creek beside his oldest son, Dr. Green Washington Hill, who had died a few months earlier.

Elizabeth Hill buried a son and husband the
same year. She was left after those tragedies to serve
as the master mind of her farm and family responsi-
bilities and duties that she faithfully performed.

It staggers the imagination to realize that this
woman had reared twelve children, moved from
Georgia to Texas, established a frontier home, lived

through two Mexican wars, and buried one son and her husband.

Elizabeth Hill demonstrated her business acumen and modernity when she placed an order with the Singer Sewing Machine Company for twelve of the new labor-saving wonders, the first to be brought into Texas. She gave one to each daughter and one to each daughter-in law.

Sometime after the death of his wife, Alexander Thompson married his long-time neighbor, Elizabeth Barksdale Hill.

Following the death of her second husband, the dowager Elizabeth moved to the home of her son, Asa Collingsworth Hill, in Thompsonville in Gonzales County and spent her last years there. In a letter of January 12, 1924, from Three Rivers, Live Oak County, W. A. Hill, son of Asa Collingsworth, wrote to my wife, Sue, stating that he remembered her living with them when he was a small child and that she died in their home.[11]

Elizabeth lived to be eighty-eight years of age, dying January 28, 1883. We have a photograph of the great lady, at just what age we aren't sure. We judge about eighty.

In a full skirted flowered dress, buckle-belted at the waist, and closed at the neck with a white collar and brooch, she sits in the classical pose beside a table, her left hand resting on the Bible, her right hand on the inseparable sewing basket on her lap. Her white bonnet, shirred around the edge, has two ribbons hanging in the customary fashion. Her face reveals tenderness and strength.

Sue and I rather imagine the dress is some

kind of flowered print of a lavender color. In our own reproduction of this photograph we have had it softly colored.

Thus it hangs in our parlour with a group of Hill relatives, Eugenia Theresa Hill Nuckols (Sue's mother), Green Washington Hill, Dr. Green Washington Hill, John Christopher Columbus Hill and others. The Hill descendants are legion!

Green Washington Hill, age 21, son of Dr. Green Washington Hill, father of Eugenia Theresa Hill Nuckols and grandfather of Sue Nuckols Bartlett. (Hill family records.)

16

Light Along the Path

S ADNESS ENTERED THE HOME of John Hill in the
death of Señora Augustina Sagredo de Hill on
June 27, 1891. His daughter Augustina had married,
and his son Carlos, who studied at Swarthmore
College, was engaged in business.[1]

For some time John's letters reflected periods
of loneliness and depression. He wrote often to his
relatives. His niece, Lucy Hill, visited him and they
kept up a steady correspondence. Another niece,
Delia came to stay with him for awhile. Delia was the
daughter of Elizabeth Louisiana Hill and William
Penn Kerr.

John kept busy with his mining operations and
investments in Mexico and the United States.

About five years passed when a beam of light
broke through the clouds that had hovered about
him. When Hamlin Garland was in Mexico, getting
data for an article to be published in *McClure's Maga-
zine*, he interviewed Dr. John C. C. Hill relative to
President Ulysses Grant's visit to that country some
years before. In the article, which was published later,

Hill's name was mentioned and also some of the incidents of his early life; among others his capture by Santa Anna's army at Mier when a boy of thirteen years of age. The article referred to came to the notice of Mrs. Masterson and Mrs. Blood in San Francisco, California, both of whom recognized in the circumstances related and in the name, the friend of their early youth.[2]

Immediately Mrs. Blood wrote to him asking him if it could be possible they were not mistaken, and if not to tell them what had become of him all these years. He replied, giving an account of himself to Mrs. Blood, and requesting her in return to write him of his old sweetheart and of her present circumstances, to which she complied.

A correspondence between the two former lovers then ensued and continued for more than a year, when they were happily united in marriage, with the full consent and blessing of her and his children.

While on their wedding trip from California to Mexico they visited Dr. Hill's brother, James Monroe Hill and family in Austin. It was then that the foregoing was related by Mrs. Mary (Masterson) Hill to Dr. John C. C. Hill's niece, who recorded it, just as it was told to her in 1898, for those others who would perhaps be interested in it in after years.

Inscribed on the business letterhead of Hickman and Masterson, 60 Calle de Market, San Francisco, California, John wrote his daughter, Maclovia, on January 22, 1900:

San Francisco
January 25, 1900

My dear daughter Cova,

I left your mother this morning at 1133 17th Street East Oakland so I could come to the city for some family business. Lila and Jessie who were living in the city of Alameda moved to this city yesterday and are living at Height Street #457 where I just was visiting them.

I am mailing this from the office of Juan Enrique (Harry Masterson), Crocker Building #25 and your new sister Jessie is now working as a cashier in the same office as your brother.

Your mother instructed me to send this letter from both of us and give you our deepest thanks for the lovely letter you sent to us on the 15th of this same month.

Since I have had to fix many things at home that we were renting out that the renters had broken I haven't had time to write to you or our friends. But now I won't be as busy and will be able to write to you with more frequency.

All your relatives and friends have sent their regards as well to your little daughters Maria and Adelina and your uncles and other relatives, particularly your cousin Lucy,

From now on send your letters to #1133 17th Street East Oakland, California as we will receive them the same but a day earlier.

Your father that loves you dearly,
John C. C. Hill[3]

We assume from this letter that John and Mary after their marriage, were living in Oakland California, possibly in the former house of the Mathesons or a new one.

John appears to be using the Matheson office. He mentions Carlos has an office there also and that Jessie Matheson is working as a cashier.

With offices in both California and Mexico, John continued to carry on his business enterprises. In journeys to Texas he always visited his relatives and neighbors.

As he traveled he wrote the homefolks about the Galveston flood, the night light displays in Chicago, Wall Street and China Town in New York. In a letter to William Webb he once wrote, "One makes friends abroad but they cannot be compared to the love of the dear ones at home."

Monterey, Mexico
November 24, 1899

Monterey de N'Leon

Our dear daughter Cova:

    We had the pleasure of receiving your nice letter directed to *both* of us, which is exactly what you should do since it is unnecessary to write to us separately as it would waste time which you could spend on more important things. For that reason your mother and I have agreed to send this letter as well as future ones from *both* of us.

We're so happy to hear you had a happy birthday and received so many gifts from your uncles, Lucy and the girls. After having gotten over the emotion and surprise that it must have caused you, you should be able to forgive them for having made you cry with happiness.

No wonder you are so happy. There is nothing in life that creates as much pleasure as that of a mother who will be able to see her children so well educated in all the essential areas that are necessary to succeed in society. Maria as well as Adelina have a lot of talent and are very applied in the essential things that will enable them to exceed in everything they are taught, and their own self-esteem will not let them fail.

Your mother is very happy that the girls liked the books we sent. The next ones will be in English so that their uncles will be able to read them.

Today we received a letter from your cousin Josie who lives in Galveston. Louisita is very advanced in her studies and especially in her music. She plays the piano and mandolin. Your cousin Georgia will arrive here next Monday between 7 and 8 o'clock in the morning. She has been in Galveston a few days visiting her sister Josie and Mrs. Glass is also there with Josie, having a good time swimming in the ocean. Josie has instructed us to tell you to go visit her with the girls for your vacation. Since it is probable that Lucy or your aunt will write to her, you can send your thanks with them.

Nothing new to tell you in this letter so I will end it sending best regards to all your relatives and kisses to both the girls and my dear Cova, you know that we love you with all our heart and wish you every happiness.

Mary Hill   John C.C. Hill

p.s. Dr. Lozanos told me that he thinks he will rent out his home and take his family to San Antonio or some other place in the United States so that his children will have a better education in English as he considers it the only way to learn a language with perfection.

Tell me what to do with the things you left there to store.

Lately Dr. Lozanos' wife has been ill for a week. She is fine now. Yesterday we went to visit her but she and the girls had gone to visit someone so we were unable to see her.

Your piano is for sale but as yet there has been no buyer.[4]

The years in Mexico, naturally, had enriched John's life. He loved the language, people, the culture. As an official of the railway system he had traveled widely. He made frequent trips to the mountains and ancient towns. He had explored historic ruins and hunted where wild game abounded.

He was privileged to know intimately many leading citizens of Mexico of diverse backgrounds: Pedro de Ampudia, professional soldier, Santa Anna, military commander and political wizard, Jose Marie

Tornel, eminent scholar and vice president, Dr. Gomez Farias, liberal who helped the Texans overthrow Santa Anna, and the Archbishop, Manuel Posada. This erudite ecclesiastic was his friend and counselor.

He also knew President Juarez and President Dias, reformers who endeavored to break the manacles that kept the peons in illiteracy and poverty.

He was exposed to the intellectual leaders of Mineria College and the University of Mexico where he made many student and faculty friends.

He lived in two countries and loved both of them advocating enlightenment and progress, cooperation and peace.

It appears that John Christopher Columbus Hill was the founder of the Good Neighbor Policy which came into vogue in later years.

Maclovia Dawe, John's daughter, wrote from Monterey February 25, 1904, to her cousin:

> My very dear Delia,
>
> With pleasure and sadness I received your two letters from the 22 and 24. I will answer them later so you can receive them before you come.
>
> I would like to write alot about dear father. When you come we can talk about it. He was only with us for 26 hours. I didn't even know that he was sick. I am very sad and miss him very much, poor father.
>
> Cousin Hettie says if you come soon she will wait because she wants to leave March 8.
>
> Thank you so much for your letters dear Delia and how happy it will be to see

you soon.

I have had many visitors that haven't left. Yesterday I wasn't able to send your letter and now I still have many visitors.

Lots of kisses to Cousin Georgia and you from Maria, Adelina and more from your cousin that loves you.

Maclovia[5]

John Christopher Columbus Hill died suddenly at Monterey at the age of seventy-five at the home of his daughter, Maclovia, on February 16, 1904. His body was laid to rest in Monterey Cemetery.

Virginia Nuckols Cason, great-great-granddaughter of Asa Hill, sister of Sue Nuckols Bartlett. Pioneer educator. (Hill family records.)

17

Remembering the Patriots

*T*HE CITIZENS OF FAYETTE COUNTY initiated a movement in September 1844 to bring the bones of
Colonel Nicholas Mosby Dawson's men who had
been murdered by the Mexicans near Salado Creek
southeast of San Antonio back to La Grange. In 1848
an effort was made to move the remains of the Mier
men who had been slaughtered March 24, 1843, at
Hacienda Salado by the Mexican firing squad. Major
Walter P. Lane was making a reconnaissance near San
Luis Potosi during the Mexican American War.
Captain John E Dusenberry, one of the survivors of
the drawing of the beans, was in this party. He persuaded the major to make a detour and secure the
remains of the Texans who had been shot and buried
there. Five of the troopers had witnessed the bean
drawing and guided the detail.

On their arrival May 3, 1847, they ordered the
alcalde to exhume the bodies. He protested and the
local priest was horrified at the thought of disturbing
the dead. Kind-hearted village women had set up a
cross and placed flowers on the resting place of their
enemies. When the earth was moved they cried,

"*Por Dios.*" The bones of the victims were packed in four large boxes and strapped on the backs of two mules. The packages were sent to the headquarters of General Zachary Taylor and were transported about Mexico with his forces until peace was declared. Captain Dusenberry was then detailed to convey them to La Grange, which had been selected because it was the former home of the ranking officer who had been shot at Hacienda Salado, Captain William Mosby Eastland, a cousin of Colonel Mosby Dawson, whose company had been slain at Salado Creek in Texas.

Dusenberry carried the bones to Galveston, and then by wagon to La Grange, where they were stored in the court house until some permanent burial spot could be established.

The remains of Dawson's troops were also brought to La Grange and interred with the Mier men in a vault on the bluff overlooking the Colorado River. On September 18, 1848, the sixth anniversary of the Dawson Massacre, many Texan veterans assembled, including Sam Houston, to pay tribute to these martyrs. Captain Dusenberry was the orator of the day.

The memorial vault fell into disrepair and a new one was dedicated September 18, 1933. In 1936 a shellstone shaft was erected at the end of the tomb This forty-eight-foot shaft is seven feet in depth and ten feet in width and rests on a terraced base of Indiana limestone. Down the full length of the face is a sculptured colored plaster designed by Pierre Bourbelle depicting the drawing of the beans and other incidents of the Mier Expedition. A ten-foot bronze statue, executed by Raoul Jesset, stands at the base of the panel before a slab of pink Texas granite. On each side of the shaft are two bronze plaques bearing the names of the Dawson and Mier men.[1]

This towering monument keeps alive the odyssey of "the heroes of the Republic of Texas who lived in this historic village."

The last name to appear chiseled in stone is:

John C. C. Hill

This name follows those of Asa Hill and Jeffrey B. Hill.

George A. Hill Jr. of Houston made an eloquent address at the dedication of this monument on December 9, 1936, entitled "The Hill Family of Fayetteville, Typical Texans." He mentioned some of the distinguished Hill men and women who were pioneers and builders of the United States of America. He spoke of Benjamin Harvey Hill, U.S. Senator from Georgia and foremost reconciliation leader during the Civil War, and a close friend of James Monroe Hill. He spoke of Izaac La Fayette Hill who served at San Jacinto, and of Willard Pinckney Hill, a federal judge.[2]

The place chosen for the monument to the Texas Veterans was called Monument Hill. This strategic location overlooks the rolling countryside along the meandering Colorado River. The hills and prairies are spotted with cedars and live oaks in their mantles of Spanish moss. Bluebonnets and other wild flowers flourish in their seasons. The pastoral community of La Grange provides an idyllic setting for this historic park.

The many stately houses, characterized by their Victorian charm of shuttered windows and spacious porches, are unusual in an early pioneer settlement which is only four thousand or so population today. Listed in Texas Houses of the Nineteenth Century is the Kaulback residence of La Grange. This house was originally built prior to 1869 in smaller size by General William G. Webb and his wife, Sarah, daughter of Asa Hill.

A second historical monument was set up in Rutersville, Texas, on October 14, 1973, in memory of Asa Hill:

Asa Hill of Rutersville
(1788?–1844)
Born in Martin County, N. C.

Married Elizabeth Barksdale in Georgia, October 6, 1808. Came to Texas in 1835. In Army in 1836, was sent by General Houston to warn people in enemy's path. Settled here 1839. In 1840, enrolled eight children In Rutersville College. With sons Jeffrey and John C. C., joined the 1842 Expedition to Mier, Mexico, captured, he drew a white bean—thus escaped death, but was in prison until August, 1843. Jeffrey was wounded, captured, likewise imprisoned. John C. C., then 14, was adopted by General Santa Anna. Asa Hill died here, was buried on Cedar Creek, Off Sh 159.
(1973)[3]

Three descendants of Asa spoke at the ceremonies: Luther Henry Hill, great-great-grandson of Asa, Asa Hill and Joseph E. Blanton, a great-great-grandson.

The adventures of the Boy Captive were acted out under six flags: the colors of the Spanish Empire, the Republic of Mexico, the Lone Star Republic, the Empire of Maximilian, the Confederate States and the United States.

The long journey of John Christopher Columbus Hill from the Lone Star Republic into the vastness of the neighboring land of the Eagle and Serpent is remembered on both sides of the border by those who admire the valor of the human spirit.

The records of the Monument Hill Ceremonies included the following tribute to the heroes of Fayette County:

> "Fayette County, well may you mourn your fallen heroes. The lot was thine to send forth that spartan band, no more to return to thee, till by weeping friends their bones were gathered from the distant field to find their last kind rest on Monument Hill. They fell! But long will they live in the hearts of their admiring countrymen. Their names stand recorded high on the historic page of their country's glory, where they still shine with undiminished lustre through countless ages and unborn generations will teach their praise.
>
> "Fayette, guard sacredly thy treasures; sons and daughters of Fayette deck with flowers their honored bier, for the rich inheritance of the happy home you now enjoy! They fell; they are gone: but long will they live in the grateful hearts of every Texan."[4]

The pageant "Texas" presented in 1936 as part of the centennial celebration of the Republic contained a dramatization of the story of John Christopher Columbus Hill.

These settlers had arrived with a set of principles. They believed in Democracy and self government exemplified by the founding fathers.

They were a cross section of the spirit of the nineteenth century, coming from Virginia, Kentucky, the Carolinas, Tennessee and Georgia. They came by ship, covered wagons and on horseback.

These people did not plan to collect gold and depart. They were willing to match their strength with the good earth and win a livelihood through their own labor.

They had sold their property and everything they owned. They came with their cash savings, a few heirlooms and their children. They crossed mountains and rivers and boundless prairies to set up their claims to a share in the unfolding American dream.

Hugh Kerr wrote a poem championing Texas independence from Mexico, the formation of a republic and entrance into the United States of America:

The Heroes of Texas
(Tune, Washington March)

1

Some nations of their heroes boast,
As England, he of Waterloo;
But we will Texas heroes toast,
For they are brave and clement too:

Then Texas heroes we will toast,
Who bravely fought the invading foe,
On the San Jacinto plain and the Alamo.

2

The heroes of the Alamo,
No Troy or Spartan band exceeds;
To San Jacinto we may go,
And there recount heroic deeds.
Then Texas' heroes we will toast,
Who bravely fought the invading foe
On the San Jacinto plain and the Alamo.

3

Remov'd, they don't degenerate,
No change their native courage knows,
Not in the torrid climate heat,
Nor in the arctic chilly snows.
Then Texas heroes we will toast,
Who bravely fought the invading foe,
On the San Jacinto plain and the Alamo.

4

The Texans will their rights maintain;
Just claims of all they do respect,
No pirate shall their friendship gain,
No proper friendship they reject.
Then Texas' heroes we will toast,
Who bravely fought the invading foe,
On the San Jacinto plain and the Alamo.

5

Heroic volunteers we toast,
Who left their friends and native home,

Their noble friendship we will boast
Who have in aid of Texas come.
Then Texas' heroes we will toast,
Who bravely fought the invading foe,
On the San Jacinto plain and the Alamo.

6

We toast our union with that land,
Where equal rights and laws obtain
No central disannuling band,
Can there our creeds or views constrain.
Then Texas' heroes we will toast,
Who bravely fought the invading foe,
On the San Jacinto plain and the Alamo.[5]

Hugh Kerr, the erudite poet, recorded the aspirations of the new-fledged republic. He sensed that San Jacinto would stand as one of the significant victories of history.

"Measured by its results , San Jacinto was one of the decisive battles of the world. The freedom of Texas won here led to annexation and to the Mexican War, resulting in the acquisition by the United States of the states of Texas, New Mexico, Arizona, Nevada, California, Utah and parts of Colorado, Wyoming, Kansas and Oklahoma, almost one-third of the present area of the American nation, nearly a million square miles of territory, changed sovereignty."[6]

Memorial to the Texas Veterans, Monument Hill Park, La Grange, Texas. (Photograph by Mary Bartlett Reynolds.)

Burton Washing. Co. Texas —
April 29th 1880 —

Mrs. Susan Hill —
Nechanitz — Fayette Co. —

Dear Sister:

Just about a month ago
I visited La Grange with the full
expectation of finding you there,
and was very much disappointed on learning you had moved
out near Leadbetter with Cousin
Mattie. I could only dispose
of 24 hours to stay in La Grange
but during this short visit, I called
on Cousin Bettie and Mrs. Lovick
Webb with the express object of in-
quiring all about you, and requested very particularly to be remembered most kindly to you, and
Cousin Mattie; regretting so

An original handwritten John C. C. Hill letter.

much not having had the pleasure of meeting you both — as
well as my dear Nephew Green
Hill, whose residence I have not
been able to find out exactly,
but understand he is living not
very far from you; please send
him and family my love.—
My dear Mother has lately been
to Houston on a visit; she took
the trip surprisingly well. It is
now only 24 hours since she returned to this place (—Bro. Will
Kerr's)—. Sister Bettie went to San
Antonio to be at the anniversary
reunion of all the old Texas veterans which was on the 21st
inst— and I believe the trip im-
proved her health; but decided
to stay a few days longer in S.
Antonio to consult a noted
phesician that Mr. Dewees high-

ly recomended—Georgia & Josie are—with Sister Bettie and will return home with her in a few days:—

My youngest Son <u>Carlos</u> is studing English and prepairing himself to go to School here in Texas—For the present I shall leave him with Mother; he is so well taken up with his numerous relatives in this Country, that I think there is no fear of his getting home sick.

In a very few days now I shall go North and expect to leave New York to return to Mexico within about one month from now.—

Before going North I shall return to Houston and stay there a few days with Bro—William Webb

to whom you may address any letters
you wish to send to me —
I am sincerely your
most affectionate Brother —

John C. C. Hill

Notes

Chapter 1   *Arrival of the Hills*
1. George A. Hill, Jr., "The Hill Family of Fayetteville - Typical Texans," address given at La Grange, Texas, December 9, 1936.
2. Personal records on John Christopher Columbus Hill kept by Eugenia Theresa Hill Nuckols.
3. *Ibid.*
4. Early family notes, Eugenia Theresa Hill Nuckols and Sue Nuckols Bartlett.

Chapter 2   *War Clouds*
1. Wilfred H. Caldicott, *Santa Anna, The Story of the Enigma Who Once Was Mexico*, Norman, University of Oklahoma Press, 1936, p. 129.
2. M. K. Wisehart, *Sam Houston, American Giant*, Washington, Robert B. Luce, 1962, p. 248 ff.
3. William H. Caldicott, *Op. cit.*
4. M. K. Wisehart, *Op. cit.*
5. Marquis James, *The Raven: Biography of Sam Houston*, New York, Grosset & Dunlap, 1929, pps. 274–5.
6. Wilfred H. Caldicott, *Op. cit.*, p. 191.
7. *Ibid.*
8. *Ibid.*

Chapter 3   *Another Summons*
1. Hugh Kerr, *Poetic Interpretation of Texas*, New York, published by the author, 1838.

2. Thomas J. Green, *Op cit.,* and Lucy Hill Jones, records on John C. C. Hill, Texas State Archives.
3. Thomas J. Green, *Op. cit.,* p. 58.
4. James L. Trueheart, *Op. cit.,* p. 129.
5. Thomas J. Green, *Op. cit.*
6. William P. Stapp, *Prisoners at Perote,* 1945.
7. Thomas J. Green, *Op. cit.*

Chapter 4   *Impatient Volunteers*
1. Thomas J. Green, *Op. cit.,* pps. 70–73.
2. *Ibid.*
3. *Ibid.,* pps. 75–76.
4. William P. Stapp, *Op. cit.*
5. *Ibid.,* pps. 81 ff.
6. *Ibid.,* pps. 79–80.
7. Hugh Kerr, *Op. cit.*
8. *Ibid.*
9. William Preston Stapp, *Op. cit.,* p. 17.
10. Thomas J. Green, *Op. cit.,* pps. 85–86.
11. Thomas J. Green, *Op. cit.*
12. Thomas J. Green, *Op. cit.*
13. Thomas J. Green, *Op. cit.*
14. *Ibid.*

Chapter 5   *Impending Encounter*
1. Thomas J. Green, *Op. cit.,* pps. 86–88.
2. *Ibid.,* pps. 88–90.
3. *Ibid.,* pps. 91–93.
4. *Ibid.,* pps. 93–94.
5. *Ibid.,* pps. 95–96.
6. *Ibid.,* pps. 97–98.
7. *Ibid.,* pps. 99–100.
8. *Ibid.,* pps. 100–103.
9. *Ibid.,* pps. 104–107.

Chapter 6   *A Daring Venture*
1. Fannie Chambers Gooch Iglehart, *Op. cit.*
2. William Preston Stapp, *Op. cit.,* p. 21.

3. Thomas W. Bell, A *Narrative of the Capture and Subsequent Sufferings of the Mier Prisoners*, New York, 1845, Waco, Texan Press, 1964, p. 29.
4. Thomas J. Green, *Op. cit.*, p. 116.
5. Thomas J. Green, *Ibid.*
6. William Preston Stapp, *Op. cit.*, pps. 19–20.
7. Thomas J. Green, *Op. cit.*
8. Lucy Hill Jones, *Hill Biographical Notes*, Texas State Archives, and Fanny C. G. Iglehart, *Op. cit.*

Chapter 7   *The Young Hero Confronts Ampudia*
1. Lucy Hill Jones records on John C. C. Hill, Texas State Archives, and Fanny C. B. Iglehart, *Op. cit.*
2. *Ibid.*
3. Thomas J. Green, *Op. cit.*, p. 114.
4. Thomas W. Bell, *Op. cit.*, p. 93.
5. Thomas J. Green, *Op. cit.* p. 110, 117.
6. Thomas J. Green, *Ibid.*

Chapter 8   *Deceit and Humiliation*
1. Thomas J. Green, *Op. cit.*, pps. 143 ff.
2. *Ibid.*, p. 163.
3. *Ibid.*, pps. 166–175.
4. Thomas J. Green, *Op. cit.*
5. William Preston Stapp, *Op. cit.* p. 43.
6. Thomas J. Green, *Op. cit.*
7. William Preston Stapp, *Op. cit.*, p. 34.
8. Thomas J. Green, *Op. cit.*, p. 169.
9. *Ibid.*, pps. 169 ff.
10. *Ibid.*, pps. 283–286.
11. Thomas J. Green, *Op. cit.*
12. *Ibid.*

Chapter 9   *John Arrives in Mexico City*
1. Fanny C. G. Iglehart, *Op. cit.*, and Lucy Hill Jones, Hill records.
2. *Ibid.*
3. *Ibid.*

4. *Ibid.*, Hill family letters verifying Iglehart's interviews with John C. C. Hill.
5. Hill family letters (Texas State Archives) verify the materials Fanny C. G. Iglehart held with John C. C. Hill.
6. *Ibid.*

Chapter 10   *Drawing of the Black Beans*
1. Thomas J. Green, *Op. cit.*, pps. 106.
2. *Ibid.*
3. *Ibid.*
4. *Ibid.*
5. William P. Stapp, *Op. cit.*
6. Fannie Iglehart, *Op. cit.*
7. Thomas J. Green, *Op. cit.*
8. Thomas J. Green, *Op. cit.*
9. Thomas J. Green, *Op. cit.*
10. Thomas J. .Green, *Op. cit.*
11. Fannie Iglehart, *Ibid*

Chapter 11   *Grim Perote Prison*
1. Waddy Thompson, *Recollections of Mexico*, New York, Wiley and Putnam, 1846, pps. 76–77.
2. Wilfred H. Caldicott, *Op. cit.*
3. Fanny Calderon de La Barca, *Life in Mexico*, Ne# York, Doubleday, 1966, pps. 32–37.
4. Waddy Thompson, *Op. cit.*, p. 147.
5. William Preston Stapp, *Op. cit.*, p. 89.
6. Waddy Thompson, *Op. cit.*, p. 217.
7. *Ibid*, p. 53.
8. *Ibid.*
9. Thomas J. Green, *Op. cit.*, p. 217.
10. Fannie Chambers Gooch Iglehart, *Op. cit.*
11. William Preston Stapp, *Op. cit.* p. 56.
12. Thomas W. Bell, *Op. cit.*, p. 44.
13. William Preston Stapp, *Op. cit.*, p. 57.
14. Thomas W. Bell, *Op. cit.*, p. 47.
15. William Preston Stapp, *Op. cit.*, pps. 85–89, and Sherman Garth, *Op. cit.*, p. 125.
16. William Preston Stapp, *Op. cit.*, p. 77.

17. Thomas J. Green, *Op. cit.*, p. 264, and Thomas w. Bell, *Op. cit.*, pps. 59–65.
18. *Ibid.*
19. *Ibid.*

Chapter 12   *Santa Anna and the Boy Captive*
  1. William P. Stapp, *Op. cit.*
  2. Waddy Thompson, *Op. cit.*
  3. *Ibid.*
  4. Thomas J. Green, *Op. cit.*
  5. *Ibid.*
  6. *Ibid.*
  7. *Ibid.*
  8. *Ibid.*
  9. *Ibid.*
 10. *Ibid.*
 11. William P. Stapp, *Op. cit.*
 12. Thomas J. Green, *Op. cit.*

Chapter 13   *The Fall of Santa Anna*
  1. William Preston Stapp, *Op. cit.*, p. 86.
  2. Wilfred H. Caldicott, *Op. cit.*
  3. *The Texas Handbook*, Austin, 1952.
  4. Donald Barr Chidsey, *Op. cit.*, pps. 101–139.
  5. Wilfred H. Caldicott, *Op. cit.*
  6. John A. Crow, *Mexico Today*, New York, Harper and Row, 1957, p. 121.
  7. William P. Stapp, *Op. cit.*, p. 101.
  8. Wilfred H. Caldicott, *Op. cit.*, and *The Handbook of Texas*.
  9. Letter, Asa Collingsworth Hill toWilliam Webb October 2, 1887.

Chapter 14   *Engineer, Entrepreneur, Physician*
  1. Early romance, John C. C. Hill and Mary Ann Murray, Lucy Hill Jones, 1898.
  2. Fanny C. G. Iglehart, *Op. cit.*
  3. *Ibid.*
  4. Lucy Hill Jones, Hill Genealogy Notes, Texas State Archives.

4a. W. H. Caldicott, *Op. cit.*
5. Caldicott, *Ibid.*
6. Letter, John C. C. Hill to Wm. Webb, September 4, 1887.
7. Letter, John C. C. Hill to Lucy Hill, November 20, 1886.
8. Letter, John C. C. Hill to Lucy Hill, June 6, 1893.
9. Letter, John C. C. Hill to Lucy Hill, November 12, 1894.
10. Letter, John C. C. Hill to Lucy Hill, December 27, 1896.
11. Letter, Asa Collingsworth Hill to his brother John, November 21, 1880.
12. Letter, Asa Collingsworth Hill to William Webb, June 7, 1886.
13. Letter, John C. C. Hill to Willie Simmons, September 13, 1901.

Chapter 15 *The Hill Family Saga*
1. Letter, Maclovia Hill to Elizabeth Hill, March 17, 1881.
2. Letter, John C. C. Hill to Maclovia Dawe, January 12, 1900.
3. Letter, Angelina Dawe to Lucy Hill, January 1, 1905.
4. Letter, Delia Kerr to John C. C. Hill, January 15, 1880.
5. Letter, John C. C. Hill to William G. Webb, September 4, 1881.
6. Letter, John C. C. Hill to Lucy Hill, September 10, 1882.
7. Letter, John C. C. Hill to Lucy Hill, November 2, 1896.
8. Letter, John C. C. Hill to William G. Webb, March 3, 1880.
9. Letter, John C. C. Hill to William G. Webb, September 27, 1880.
10. George A. Hill, Jr., "The Hill Family of Fayetteville - Typical Texans," 1936.
11. Hill family records.

Chapter 16 *Light Along the Path*
1. Death certificate, Monterey, Mexico, June 7, 1891, for Señora Augustina Segredo Hill.
2. Early romance of John C. C. Hill and Mary Ann Murray, Lucy Hill Jones, 1898.
3. Letter, San Francisco, January 25, 1900, John C. C. Hill to Maclovia Dawe.
4. Letter, Monterey, November 24, 1899, John C. C. Hill to Maclovia Dawe.

5. Letter, Monterey, February 25, 1904, Maclovia Dawe to
    Delia Kerr.

Chapter 17   *Remembering the Patriots*
1. Monument Hill Memorial, La Grange, Texas, 1936.
2. George A. Hill, Jr., "The Hill Family - Typical Texans,"
    address and dedication of Monument Hill Memorial,
    1935.
3. Asa Hill Monument, erected by his descendants,
    Rutersville, Texas, 1973. For family background see *Isaac
    Hill and His Descendants*, by Lennon Hill and Marie
    Weston Hill, 3706 42nd St., Lubbuck, Texas 79413, 1981.
    The remains of Asa Hill and his son, Dr. Green Washing-
    ton Hill, were reburied in the La Grange Cemetery in 1975
    among the graves of their relations, the Webbs, Blantons,
    and others.
4. Dedicatory statement for Monument Hill Memorial 1936.
5. Hugh Kerr, *A Poetic Interpretation of Texas*, New York. 1838.
6. Publication of the San Jacinto Museum of History
    Association.